Indefinite Reenlistment and Noncommissioned Officers

Laura Miller, Joy S. Moini, Suja Sivadasan,
Jennifer Kavanagh, Miriam Shergold,
Ronald Plasmeijer

Prepared for the Office of the Secretary of Defense

 NATIONAL DEFENSE RESEARCH INSTITUTE

The research described in this report was prepared for the Office of the Secretary of Defense (OSD). The research was conducted in the RAND National Defense Research Institute, a federally funded research and development center sponsored by the OSD, the Joint Staff, the Unified Combatant Commands, the Department of the Navy, the Marine Corps, the defense agencies, and the defense Intelligence Community under Contract W74V8H-06-C-0002.

Library of Congress Cataloging-in-Publication Data

Indefinite reenlistment and noncommissioned officers / Laura Miller ... [et al.].
    p. cm.
    Includes bibliographical references.
    ISBN 978-0-8330-4043-5 (pbk. : alk. paper)
    1. United States—Armed Forces—Recruiting, enlistment, etc. 2. United States.
Army—Non-commissioned officers—Recruiting, enlistment, etc.
I. Miller, Laura L., 1967– II. Rand Corporation.

    UB323.I54 2007
    355.2'2362—dc22

2007002184

Published 2007 by the RAND Corporation
1776 Main Street, P.O. Box 2138, Santa Monica, CA 90407-2138
1200 South Hayes Street, Arlington, VA 22202-5050
4570 Fifth Avenue, Suite 600, Pittsburgh, PA 15213-2665
RAND URL: http://www.rand.org/
To order RAND documents or to obtain additional information, contact
Distribution Services: Telephone: (310) 451-7002;
Fax: (310) 451-6915; Email: order@rand.org

Preface

Enlisted military personnel in the U.S. Armed Forces typically commit to a series of fixed-period enlistment contracts from initial enlistment until the point of retirement. In the early 1990s, a U.S. Army study found that most senior enlisted Army personnel preferred an indefinite reenlistment (IR) status that would allow them to serve until retirement without having to reenlist periodically. The Army's expectation was that implementation of indefinite reenlistment would improve soldiers' morale and sense of professionalism while reducing personnel processing costs associated with contract renewals. The Army therefore sponsored legislation that was passed by Congress in 1996 authorizing indefinite reenlistment in all the military services. To date, however, only the Army has chosen to implement such a program.

In 2003, the Office of the Deputy Under Secretary of Defense for Personnel and Readiness asked the RAND National Defense Research Institute to evaluate the Army's experience with indefinite reenlistments in terms of the satisfaction of noncommissioned officers (NCOs) and to assess the potential costs and benefits of implementation in the other services. In response to that call, the RAND Corporation undertook a review of reenlistment policies in each of the U.S. Armed Services and in several Western militaries, and also examined the Army's indefinite reenlistment program to determine its impact on the service and to evaluate whether the other services should reconsider the introduction of indefinite reenlistment.

This study should be of interest to military personnel policymakers in the Office of the Secretary of Defense as well as those in each of the military services as they revisit the possibility of adopting a policy of indefinite reenlistment.

This research was sponsored by the Office of the Deputy Under Secretary of Defense for Personnel and Readiness and conducted within the Forces and Resources Policy Center of the RAND National Defense Research Institute, a federally funded research and development center sponsored by the Office of the Secretary of Defense, the Joint Staff, the Unified Combatant Commands, the Department of the Navy, the Marine Corps, the defense agencies, and the defense Intelligence Community.

For more information on RAND's Forces and Resources Policy Center, contact the director, James Hosek. He can be reached by email at James_Hosek@rand.org; by phone at 310-393-0411, extension 7183; or by mail at the RAND Corporation, 1776 Main Street, Santa Monica, California 90407-2138. More information about RAND is available at www.rand.org.

Contents

Figure

Tables

Summary

The Army Pioneered Indefinite Reenlistment in the United States

In 1998, the Army shifted its senior enlisted force from a fixed enlistment contract system to indefinite reenlistment. The stated intention was to recognize senior NCOs as career soldiers and thereby increase their prestige. The Army program was designed to meet this goal by eliminating the reenlistment requirement in the latter half of the NCO's career and by placing senior NCOs on the same indefinite service contract as officers. Over 90 percent of soldiers with a rank of E-6 or higher with ten or more years of service remain in the Army until retirement. The indefinite reenlistment policy requires all soldiers reaching the rank of E-6 with ten years of service to reenlist indefinitely. Their new separation date becomes either the year they are required to leave the service if not promoted or their retirement date, whichever occurs first. Soldiers may self-initiate separation if they have met all other service obligations through moves, schooling, retraining, or deployment. This program mirrors the management of officers and eliminates the need for career NCOs to repeatedly fill out reenlistment paperwork. The Army is satisfied with the program and has no plans to change it. This monograph presents the findings of the first study of the Army's program to determine whether it has met its primary goals, namely increasing the prestige of the NCO corps.

The Other Services Have Rejected Indefinite Reenlistment

The Navy, Marine Corps, and Air Force could have adopted similar programs following congressional approval in 1997, but each considered and then rejected open-ended enlistments. Their primary concerns were that force planning would be more difficult if troops' actual separation dates were unpredictable, that the quality of the NCO corps would drop if the reenlistment screening mechanism were eliminated, and that retention of senior NCOs with critical skills would suffer because of the loss of reenlistment bonuses. Furthermore, these services were concerned that NCO morale would drop, rather than increase, because service members would lose benefits, bargaining power, and the meaningful ceremonies that accompany reenlistment.

Focus Group Participants Argue That Indefinite Reenlistment Is Undesirable and Not Linked to Retention

Although Army NCO continuation rates were relatively unchanged during the transition to indefinite reenlistment, focus group data suggest some confusion and dissatisfaction with the program among senior enlisted personnel. The NCOs we were able to interview believed that indefinite reenlistment did not boost prestige, and the junior enlisted personnel were generally unaware that their leaders were not serving under shorter-term fixed contracts similar to their own. Soldiers perceived the policy as one that restricts their options as they gain seniority and knowledge in exchange for a negligible reduction in reenlistment paperwork.

Focus groups with Navy, Marine Corps, and Air Force personnel revealed objections to the implementation of indefinite reenlistment status for their senior enlisted officers. Sailors and Marines reported that their senior NCOs already enjoyed a high level of prestige, and that they had no desire for NCOs' terms of service to mimic those of officers. Service members from each of these branches also raised concerns that indefinite reenlistment would retain poor performers and reduce promotion and leadership opportunities for quality junior personnel. Marines in particular said they would lament the loss of the reenlistment ceremony, a significant ritual of service commitment. Air Force personnel were concerned about the loss of reenlistment bonuses for people they believed to have earned them the most. None of the focus group participants felt that the reenlistment process was burdensome or worth the potential negative consequences of shifting to indefinite reenlistment.

Despite the generally negative opinion of the indefinite reenlistment program, none of the service members in our study said that an indefinite service contract did or would influence their decision to reenlist or remain in the military.

Indefinite Reenlistment Has Little to Offer as a Force Management Tool

Consideration of possible functions that indefinite reenlistment might play in force management reveals no significant improvement or cost savings relative to tools currently available in each of the services for managing recruitment, retention, skill mix, or size of the force.

This study recommends that the Navy, Marine Corps, and Air Force continue their current reenlistment programs for senior NCOs. There is no evidence, however, that the Army's program is producing any degree of harm that warrants reversion to fixed contracts; therefore, we also recommend adherence to the status quo for the Army's senior reenlistment policy.

Acknowledgments

This work benefited from the support and guidance of Lt. Col. Tim Donohue, Bradford Loo, Gwen Rutherford, and especially project monitor Maj. Harvey Johnson of the Office of the Deputy Under Secretary of Defense for Military Personnel Policy. We are grateful to Lt. Col. Charles Armentrout (USAF) for coordinating focus groups with Air Force personnel, George Thompson for arranging focus groups with Army personnel, and LCDR Mark Edwards (USN) for coordinating focus groups with Marines and Navy service members.

We wish to thank our military contacts from Australia, Austria, Belgium, Canada, France, Germany, the Netherlands, and the United Kingdom for their generous assistance with the international reviews. In particular, we are grateful to Lt. Col. Didier Speleers and Col. Carlo Wouters (recently retired) of the Belgium Army; Col. François Philbert, French military attaché to London; Dr. J. A. M. Komen, head of Communication and Human Resources of the Royal Dutch Army; and Lt. Col. Bob Hamilton and Maj. Alastair Harvey of the British Army. We would also like to thank Doug Lock, manager of Military Human Resources Policy Development and director of Military Employment Policy for the Department of National Defence Canadian Forces; Lee Roberts, Canadian director of general workforce planning, recruitment, and retention; and Brian Adams, head of Defence Personnel Executive for the Australian Department of Defence, for providing important information about the enlisted personnel systems in their respective countries.

We acknowledge the contributions of Laura Castaneda, who conducted focus groups with enlisted personnel, and Jill Gurvey and Mark Totten, who computed Army continuation rates before and after indefinite reenlistment. Susan Everingham, Meg Harrell, and Jim Hosek offered valuable insights and project guidance. Dina Levy provided project guidance and extensive editing on many drafts of the manuscript. Al Robbert, Gery Ryan, and Mike Schiefer reviewed the draft manuscript and helped elevate the level of analysis in the final document. Finally, we appreciate the administrative assistance from Janie Christensen, Shirley Cromb, and Linda Walgamott.

Abbreviations

AFS	Active Federal Service
CAN	Center for Naval Analysis
CE	Continuing Engagement
CF	Canadian Forces
CJR	Career Job Reservation
DA	Department of the Army
DCSPER	Deputy Chief of Staff for Personnel
DFAS	Defense Finance and Accounting Service
DOD	[Australian] Department of Defence
DoD	Department of Defense
ENLOP	Enlistment Option
EREC	Enlisted Records and Evaluation Center
ETS	Expiration of Term of Service
FCMS	Flexible Career Management System
FFM	Fast Filling Military Occupational Specialty
FY	Fiscal Year
HQDA	Headquarters, Department of the Army

IAW	In Accordance With
IE25	Intermediate Engagement 25
IPS	Indefinite Period of Service
IR	Indefinite Reenlistment
MCP	Manning Control Point
MOS	Military Occupational Specialty
NC	Navy Career Counselors
NCO	Noncommissioned Officer
NDAA	National Defense Authorization Act
NDRI	National Defense Research Institute
ODCSPER	Office of the Deputy Chief of Staff for Personnel
PDUSD(P&R)	Principal Deputy Under Secretary of Defense for Personnel and Readiness
PERSCOM	Personal Command
POC	Point of Contact
QMP	Qualitative Management Program
RA	Regular Army
RCP	Retention Control Point
RETAIN	Reenlistment and Reclassification
RIF	Reduction in Force
SERB	Selective Early Retirement Board
SPCMA	Special Court—Martial Authority
SRB	Selective Reenlistment Bonus
TOS	Term of Service

TRS	Time Remaining in Service
UCMJ	Uniform Code of Military Justice
USAF	U.S. Air Force
VENG	Versatile Engagement
VIE	Variable Initial Engagement

CHAPTER ONE

Introduction

The personnel branches of the armed services strive to retain enough high-quality enlisted personnel with the experience, training, education, and leadership skills required to support their service missions. *Force management policies* are designed to help the services plan and achieve an optimal force structure within legal and fiscal constraints. Simultaneously, *career management policies* aim to ensure viable and equitable career opportunities that meet the preferences of service members.

The services implement a variety of tools to shape the size and composition of the force. For example, enlistment and reenlistment bonuses and expedited promotions can increase the number of personnel overall or in specific occupations, while decreases can be achieved through voluntary and involuntary early retirement or separation or through opportunities to retrain and change occupations. Indefinite reenlistment, another such tool, leaves enlistment status open ended for career noncommissioned officers (NCOs) until retirement. This continuous status, currently adopted in the United States only by the Army, contrasts with a series of fixed enlistment contracts that may or may not last until retirement. This tool is relatively new to the all-volunteer force, because Congress did not authorize it until 1996.

Origins of the Indefinite Reenlistment Policy Option

Prior to 1998, each branch of the all-volunteer force offered fixed contracts for enlisted personnel throughout their careers. Reenlistment was determined by the intersection of the needs of each service and service members' preferences. Traditionally, the end of the enlistment contract has served as a point at which the services shed poor performers, manage under- and overfilled jobs, and expand or contract the enlisted force through incentives or cutbacks.

A 1992 study for the Army's Deputy Chief of Staff for Personnel (DCSPER) examined the option of introducing mandatory indefinite reenlistment for career soldiers.[1] The Army study reportedly included five focus groups with approximately five NCOs in each, divided by years of service. The advantages of indefinite reenlistment cited by focus group participants were "increase in soldiers' sense of control over career," "more prestige for NCOs," and "easier than going through the reenlistment process, which can be a hassle" (Peck and Martin, 1995, p. 67). The disadvantages mentioned included loss of reenlistment bonuses, "cultural change/procedural upheaval," and "need to make a career decision at one point in time" (Peck and Martin, 1995, p. 67). A Navy-sponsored summary of the Army study did not report whether the NCOs themselves were in favor of indefinite reenlistment.

The Army study recommended an indefinite reenlistment policy for soldiers who achieve the rank of E-6 and who have at least ten years of service. The report recommended that upon attaining indefinite reenlistment status, soldiers incur a three-year service obligation and then serve "at will," although training, change of station, and promotion would add further obligation. The recommended program would allow either the soldier or the Army to initiate separation prior to retirement:

---

[1] The Army's copy of the study report, "U.S. Army's Enlisted Voluntary Indefinite Status Versus Reenlistment Periods Study," New York: PRC Inc. and MTL Services, International, Inc., August 1993, was destroyed in the September 11, 2001, attack on the Pentagon, and RAND's National Defense Research Institute (NDRI) was unable to locate any other copies. Thus, we draw heavily on a description of the study in a subsequent report for the Navy (Peck and Martin, 1995).

> The soldier may remain on active duty in indefinite status until he reaches high-year tenure, decides to resign or retire, or until Army mandates his separation or retirement. Army may require a soldier who has entered indefinite status to separate for poor duty performance or because of a reduction in force size. (Peck and Martin, 1995, p. 9)

In addition to the expectation that indefinite reenlistment would enhance the status and prestige of NCOs, the Army-sponsored study predicted savings of $14.3 million through the elimination of selective reenlistment bonuses for careerists, along with $18 million to $26 million in personnel processing costs associated with the approximately ten pages of paperwork and up to six interviews per person required for reenlistment at that time (Peck and Martin, 1995, pp. 2, 60).[2]

In October 1993, the DCSPER approved a recommendation to develop congressional legislation for an enlisted indefinite status. According to the Navy-sponsored study's summary of the Army process at the time:

> The Army has justified the need for an [indefinite reenlistment] program *primarily* on the basis of increasing the prestige of its noncommissioned officers. The Army asserted that it is degrading for its senior enlisted personnel to have to request reenlistment from officers that in many cases have much less time in service. The Army also thinks that [indefinite reenlistment] will increase the prestige of their senior enlisted by increasing the distinction between the Army enlisted ranks, i.e., E-5 and below, and E-6 and above. (Peck and Martin, 1995, pp. 30–31)

The Army's recommendation was included in the fiscal year 1997 Defense Authorization Bill. The cover letter that accompanied the draft of the legislation sent to the Speaker of the House explained its purpose:

---

[2]   The Navy-sponsored study is critical of the Army study's methods for calculating the savings of personnel processing and says that the estimated savings were inflated.

This proposal would eliminate the administrative efforts and associated costs that occur as a consequence of the requirement to reenlist continually senior enlisted members. . . . The paperwork for reenlistment and its processing is not burdensome but it is not insignificant. Savings should result. The proposal would also increase the prestige of the noncommissioned officer corps. (Peck and Martin, 1995, pp. 41–42)

Upon the bill's approval, House Armed Services Committee Chairman Floyd D. Spence later reasserted the intent of the program:

The committee realizes that senior NCOs are generally committed to military service and have chosen a military career. To distinguish these individuals from junior enlisted and to reward their dedication to service, the committee recommends a provision that will authorize the Service Secretaries to reenlist NCOs with 10 or more years of service for indefinite periods of time. (Current law requires reenlistment for periods of a minimum of two but not more than six years.) In addition, this provision will remove an administrative irritant and an obstacle to the recognition of their increased status and importance.[3]

Objective

In 2003, the Office of the Principal Deputy Under Secretary of Defense for Personnel and Readiness (PDUSD [P&R]) asked the RAND Corporation's National Defense Research Institute (NDRI) to examine the subject of indefinite reenlistment, both in the Army and in the other services. Using the Army program as a benchmark, this study aims to provide the PDUSD(P&R) with recommendations regarding the advisability of continuing and expanding a policy of indefinite reen-

---

[3] Floyd D. Spence, "Statement of Chairman Floyd D. Spence at the Conclusion of the Mark-Up for the Fiscal Year 1997 National Defense Authorization Act," statement to the U.S. House of Representatives, http://www.house.gov/hasc/openingstatementsandpressreleases/104thcongress/markupb.htm.

listment with respect to two goals: increasing the prestige of NCOs and managing the force in a more reliable, efficient, and cost-effective manner.

Approaches

NDRI evaluated the Army's experience with its program thus far and studied the reenlistment programs of the Navy, Marine Corps, and Air Force. To review the Army's indefinite reenlistment program, we began by interviewing human resources representatives in the Army and also examined program documentation and analyzed overall continuation rates for Army personnel before and after program implementation.

We also examined documents and interviewed retention experts from the Navy, Marine Corps, and Air Force about their services' previous considerations of an indefinite reenlistment program. We asked whether reconsideration of such a policy would be appropriate in the current climate. Following this stage of research, we developed a list of policy pros and cons and prepared a protocol for learning the perspective of enlisted personnel on the issue.

Focus groups explored the appeal of indefinite reenlistment with junior and senior enlisted personnel in each U.S. service (see Appendix A for a sample focus group guide used for Air Force focus groups).[4] Enlisted personnel were asked specifically about how the policy would or did affect NCOs' morale, prestige, and professionalism. Troops sometimes volunteered but were not specifically asked to consider the effect of indefinite reenlistment on force shaping or personnel management. Focus group participants were invited to suggest how the components of indefinite reenlistment could be tailored, if desired, to better suit their service: for example, at what rank or year of service it should begin. Finally, we asked for other ways the services could improve the status and satisfaction of senior NCOs.

---

[4] The protocol varied somewhat across focus groups according to the relevance of issues to each group.

Focus group participants included 23 Army enlisted person-nel—13 in grades E-4–E-6 and 10 in grades E-7–E-9; 39 sailors (21 in E-3–E-6, 18 in E-7–E-8); 43 Marines (21 in E-3–E-5, 22 in E-6–E-9); and 43 airmen (21 in E-4–E-6, 22 in E-7–E-9). We met with junior enlisted personnel separately from career NCOs because our focus was somewhat different for those deciding whether to make the service a career than it was for those who had already made such a decision. Par-ticipation in the focus groups was voluntary, and focus group facilita-tors promised participants that any statements they made would not be attributed to them in any report. The focus groups met from an hour and a half to two hours, and either the focus group facilitator or a dedi-cated note taker took notes by hand during the sessions. We modified the previously developed list of pros and cons to include the unantici-pated points raised by interviewed personnel. That list formed the basis for the categories used to analyze these qualitative data.

From an overall analysis of the data from each of these sources, we evaluate the advisability of such a policy for the services.

Employment of Indefinite Reenlistment by Western Volunteer Militaries

Additionally, we completed a brief overview of international examples of indefinite reenlistment programs to learn about alternative ways of structuring timing, benefits, and status qualifications. We interviewed contacts in the militaries of nine Western countries with volunteer forces: Australia, Austria, Belgium, Canada, France, Germany, Italy, the Netherlands, and the United Kingdom. The evaluations of the international programs are a possible source of ideas for improving or extending the approach in place in the Army.

Indefinite reenlistment in some form was found in Australia, Aus-tria, Belgium, Canada, France, Germany, the Netherlands, and the United Kingdom. One of the primary ways in which these nations' programs differ from that of the U.S. Army is that indefinite reen-listment status is not automatic for the entire enlisted population on reaching a given rank and length of service. Many foreign programs require screening of each applicant among a group of peers through some form of examination or selection. Those who do not earn indefinite reenlistment status leave the military or continue to serve on fixed contracts without the security of employment until retirement. In this way, part of the force is selected for a career status that must be earned and that typically comes with greater benefits than those offered fixed-term enlistees.

One significant difference between the American services and those of other nations is that the American services have a 20-year retirement system, which most of their Western counterparts do not. Thus, the programs were not directly applicable to the U.S. case. Should the U.S. Department of Defense implement recent recommendations to change the American retirement program, the foreign military examples might become more relevant as ways to screen and retain quality senior enlisted personnel. The foreign military experience also warns that an indefinite reenlistment program coupled with a retirement program more similar to that of civilians can produce a force with too many older people at the top of the structure. The proper balance between the percentage of the force on career terms versus those on fixed terms must be managed on an ongoing basis to account for shifts in attrition, retention, and recruitment rates. For readers interested in these alternatives, an overview of such programs is provided in Appendix D.

Organization of This Report

Chapter Two reviews the origins and characteristics of the Army's implementation of an indefinite reenlistment program; outlines the Navy, Marine Corps, and Air Force reenlistment programs; and explains why the latter three services did not adopt an indefinite reenlistment program. Chapter Three assesses, primarily from the viewpoint of service members, indefinite reenlistment as a program beneficial for career NCOs—the stated motivation behind creation of the Army's indefinite reenlistment program. Chapter Four analyzes indefinite reenlistment as a force management tool and potential cost-saving measure for the services. Chapter Five offers conclusions and recommendations.

CHAPTER TWO

The Army Indefinite Reenlistment Program and Other Service Evaluations

On October 1, 1998, the U.S. Army implemented its indefinite reenlistment program, mandatory for every soldier who reenlists after achieving the rank of E-6 or serving on active duty for ten years. An Army memo[1] from August 18, 1998 (see Appendix A), declared:

> The indefinite reenlistment program is a positive step by the Army to permit career soldiers the opportunity to manage their careers more effectively without the unnecessary burden of renewing their contract every few years. Once on indefinite status, most soldiers will have the peace of mind that they will be permitted to serve until minimum retirement eligibility or longer, consistent with the retention control point (RCP) for their rank.

Appendixes A, B, and C contain Army announcements explaining the final design of the program and its processing procedures. Retention control points, the points at which a service member must be promoted or leave the service ("high year tenure," in other service parlance), now double as the expiration of term of service (ETS) for these career soldiers. Once reenlisted in the indefinite reenlistment, soldiers may request voluntary separation or retirement in a manner similar to officers: They must first meet any service obligations linked to deployment, schooling, training, or moving to a new post and must

---

[1] Memo provided to us by the Army G-1 (Office of the Deputy Chief of Staff for Personnel).

submit the request six months prior to the desired separation date. Soldiers who do not want to accept their next assignment can request separation within 30 days of receiving that assignment, but stop-loss provisions can remove the option to separate, even if all obligations have been met. No minimum service obligation tied to indefinite reenlistment was named.

Implementation occurred six years after the initiation of the Army-sponsored study that led to the policy change. At the time of the study, the Army was undergoing a dramatic post–Cold War drawdown; by the time indefinite reenlistment was implemented, deployments had become commonplace due to missions in places like Somalia, Haiti, Rwanda, and Bosnia. Yet an Army News Service article shortly preceding the program reveals that the Army had retaken the pulse of its enlisted force and continued to receive a positive response (Gilmore, 1998). An Army spokesperson was quoted:

> Response from the field has been overwhelmingly favorable. "The program was very well received by groups of soldiers I talked to in Europe, notably in Germany, Bosnia and Belgium," Pionk said. "In fact, I got some phone calls from soldiers saying, 'It is about time senior NCOs are given the type of prestige and status commensurate with their duties and responsibilities.'"

The Army representative quoted in the piece asserted that career NCOs would be able to petition for separation, but he did not expect many to do so because career reenlistment rates at the time averaged 93 percent.

Evidence of dissent appeared as early as 2001. A command sergeant major addressed his peers in the Winter issue of *The NCO Journal* about his concern that "what was once a popular program among some NCOs now has some unsure if indefinite reenlistment is the right way to confirm their commitment to the military" (Clifford, 2001, p. 21). The author criticized his peers who hesitated to reenlist for an indefinite term because they feared they would not be allowed to separate prior to retirement if they desired. His answer was that NCOs should be committed to a career in the Army, and he chastised those who imagined themselves leaving before completing 20 years of service.

Today, as part of the mandatory transition to indefinite reenlistment status for all those who are eligible, soldiers sign the following statement:

> I understand that my reenlistment is for an indefinite period and that I will be allowed to serve up to the retention control point for my current rank. The retention control point for my current rank is YY/MM/DD. I further understand that if I am selected for promotion/promoted, reduced in rank or become ineligible for continued service that I may be further retained or separated [in accordance with] appropriate policies in effect at the time as prescribed by the Secretary of the Army or applicable law. (Quoted from document in Appendix C)

Notably, this statement does not mention the conditions under which a soldier can initiate separation from the service. As we report later in this chapter and in the following chapter, some soldiers are unaware that they have the ability to initiate separation. Among soldiers who are aware of their right to apply for separation, some do not have a clear enough understanding of the conditions under which they are eligible to separate. An Army representative reported to us that about 10 percent of those who had applied for separation by October 2003 did not meet the criteria. The soldiers rejected for separation had remaining active duty service obligations (which enlisted personnel incur following relocation, promotion, or attendance at the Sergeants Major Academy), and their request packets did not contain any justification of hardships or extenuating circumstances that might warrant a waiver.

The effects of implementation on actual separation behavior have been minimal or nonexistent. Between October 1998 and October 2003, of all NCOs serving under the indefinite reenlistment program (those who reenlisted following ten years of service and ranking E-6 or higher), only 478 ever requested separation, and the Army has not processed a single involuntary separation under its separation provision (AR 635-200, Chapter 4, paragraph 4-4.)[2] In fact, the personnel

---

[2] A representative from the Army G-1 office provided this information.

demands for operations in Iraq and Afghanistan have resulted in a variety of stop-loss policies for Army personnel that nullify this option while in place.

The Army personnel representatives we interviewed recalled that prior to the institution of indefinite reenlistment, some leaders expressed concern that soldiers might leave the military rather than going on indefinite reenlistment. The issue was whether the long time horizon might prove daunting. One representative said the Army undertook an aggressive education program at the time to assure people that they were not signing a ten-year contract that could not be broken. The Army representative was confident that no change in retention or reenlistments had occurred, but no reports supporting that conclusion could be found because Army analyses of actual retention and reenlistment rates from before and after the implementation of indefinite reenlistment were destroyed in the attack on the Pentagon on September 11, 2001. To compensate for missing personnel data, we examined the continuation rates of soldiers who would have qualified for indefinite reenlistment before implementation of the program in 1998 and the rates of those who have qualified since.[3]

We conducted a longitudinal examination of the continuation rates of senior enlisted personnel from ranks E-6 to E-8, each with from 10 to 20 years of service, during the period from 1991 to 2000. This examination revealed no anomalies at or surrounding the 1998 shift to mandatory indefinite reenlistment status.[4] The continuation rates for NCOs before and after the program change are similar, and in most cases they seem to follow a declining trend that began prior to 1998.

The elimination of administrative reenlistment points has also removed an opportunity for soldiers to "sell back leave." Soldiers have

---

[3]   The Enlisted Master File contains the necessary information and time frame in a standardized form. This data file is derived from the Department of the Army information base for enlisted personnel management and strength accounting.

[4]   Due to limitations on project resources, we did not extend our analysis of continuation rates beyond the year 2000, when the data format was changed. For the same reason, we did not perform statistical analyses on the data after descriptive statistics suggested that no notable change occurred in 1998, 1999, or 2000.

historically been able to cash in a limited number of unused vacation days at reenlistment and retirement. Because there is no reenlistment opportunity and no other provision for doing so has yet been made, these sell-back opportunities have been eliminated for senior enlisted personnel. Thus soldiers under indefinite status will not receive compensation for any leave days beyond the accrual maximum of 60. Senior enlisted service members in the other services, where an indefinite reenlistment policy is not in place, have opportunities to receive cash for unused leave that their Army counterparts do not have.

Soldiers' Lack of Awareness or Understanding of the Indefinite Reenlistment Program

We discuss in more detail the findings of focus groups with soldiers in the next chapter, but one finding worth noting here is that we observed a range of awareness and understanding of the specific terms of indefinite reenlistment. Most junior enlisted soldiers in the focus groups were either completely unaware of the Army's indefinite reenlistment program or exhibited misconceptions about the details of the program. Some thought that making a long-term commitment to the Army at ten years of service was too much, too early. Because most junior enlisted personnel were unaware of the program, though, it was clearly not operating as a factor in their perceptions of the prestige of senior enlisted service members.

Even some senior enlisted personnel were unaware of the separation policy—i.e., that they can initiate separation after all their service obligations are met. An example of misperception is illustrated by the following exchange in one of our focus groups between two sergeants first class (E-7A and E-7B):

> E-7A: If you wanted out, you could put in a request. But I think the enlistment is binding—like a contract for ten years.

E-7B: It's an obligation—a written agreement between you and the Army. There are still ways to get out, though, like hardship, or if you get in trouble.

E-7A: You can try to get out if you come into some big money. There are special cases.

E-7B: But you can't just leave—you'd be subject to UCMJ [the Uniform Code of Military Justice].

As noted earlier, the perception that indefinite reenlistment is a ten-year contract that can be broken only under exceptional circumstances is incorrect.

Navy Consideration of Indefinite Reenlistment

In 1981 the Navy considered open-ended reenlistment contracts for personnel at the ranks of E-7 to E-9 with 15 years of experience. Those parameters were chosen because continuation rates beyond the 16-year point were consistently high and were expected to remain high under indefinite reenlistment. The Navy believed the main advantage of introducing indefinite reenlistment was prestige enhancement for the NCO corps because, like officers, upon completion of their 15th year of service they would be able to serve until retirement. However, the Navy had some concerns about introducing indefinite reenlistment. The main disadvantages from the Navy's perspective were loss of opportunity for enlisted personnel to sell back leave; the assumption that indefinite reenlistment would cancel other service obligations related, for example, to submarine pay;[5] and negative effects on sea duty manning because personnel might choose to separate from the service rather than perform certain types of sea duty. Navy leaders also consid-

---

[5] "Open-Ended Reenlistment Contracts," memorandum to the Chief of Naval Operations, February 10, 1981.

ered an informal survey of two dozen Chiefs, which revealed concerns that senior enlisted personnel would not be able to retire when they wanted or could be separated for arbitrary reasons. The Office of Naval Operations recommended that prior to implementation, the service conduct a survey of enlisted personnel to gauge the potential reaction to indefinite reenlistment and identify the administrative regulations that would be affected.[6] We were unable to determine whether such a survey was ever conducted. Regardless, the Navy did not adopt a policy of indefinite reenlistment at that time.

In 1995 the Chief of Naval Personnel revisited the issue of indefinite reenlistment. He requested a review of the Army's 1993 study of indefinite reenlistment and an evaluation of the potential effects of such a program on the Navy. The study examined the possibility of indefinite reenlistment at different career points, including after first enlistment, at 11 years of service (where retention rates first exceed 90 percent), and at 16 years of service (where retention rates are high and sailors are no longer eligible for enlistment bonuses). As in 1981, the Navy was concerned about the effects of indefinite reenlistment on retention and morale, personnel management, manning, and bonuses. The model introducing indefinite status after the first enlistment was rejected due to the expectation that it would complicate Navy personnel planning, require new behavioral models, and potentially lead to the loss of good sailors due to easier sailor-initiated separation. The 11-years-of-service option was rejected because of projected morale decline linked to loss of the reenlistment ceremony and the potential loss of sailors in critical skills, again due to the ease of separation. The model for 16 years was presented as least disruptive, but not sufficiently beneficial to be worth the risks associated with changing the policy (Peck and Martin, 1995).

The Navy report raised the issue of NCO morale and prestige, but did not consider it in any systematic way. It noted that senior enlisted personnel already enjoy distinctions and privileges, such as different uniforms and special sleep and mess accommodations aboard the ship

---

[6] "Open-Ended Reenlistment Contracts," memorandum to the Chief of Navy Personnel, February 10, 1981.

when on sea duty. The report also mentioned the importance of the reenlistment ceremony to many enlisted personnel, suggesting that there would be a negative response if it were eliminated. The study contended that indefinite reenlistment probably would not have a negative effect on retention as long as selective reenlistment bonuses were preserved. However, dramatic increases in retention would not be expected either.

Regarding the opportunity to sell back leave, the report authors noted that under indefinite reenlistment, personnel could still potentially sell back leave at three points during their career: at the end of their first two contract periods and when they retire under indefinite status. Because personnel are currently not allowed to sell back more than 60 days over the length of their career, those three opportunities could be considered sufficient. Special pay was also addressed in the 1995 report. In particular, the Navy expressed concern about the effects of indefinite reenlistment contracts on submarine sailors who receive special pay during shore duty in exchange for 14 months of obligated service on sea duty. The report concludes that a special agreement could be made under indefinite reenlistment to still obligate recipients of special pay. An agreement would require a change in the administrative instructions but could be done easily, according to the study.

Finally, the Navy study looked at the reduction in the administrative burden of processing reenlistment contracts and determined that it would be minimal. Although some reenlistment paperwork would be reduced, the report says, "it is doubtful that any real dollar savings would accrue" because the change would not be large enough to warrant a reduction in billets for Navy career counselors (NCs) (Peck and Martin, 1995, p. 30). An estimate of savings was not included in the report. However, reenlistment counseling and paperwork for senior enlisted personnel are considered a small part of an NC's duties. In addition, the report suggested that paperwork requirements for the indefinite reenlistment program could offset any cost savings that would otherwise accrue. Overall, the conclusion of the 1995 study was that the advantages did not outweigh the disadvantages of implementing indefinite reenlistment, but if the policy were to be adopted, implementation at 11 years of service would be the best compromise between the desire to minimize disruption to the personnel system and the goal to save on the processing of reenlistments (under this option, two to three per career soldier).

Interviews we conducted in February 2004 with three Navy staff members in the Office of the Assistant Secretary of the Navy, Manpower Analysis, and Assessment and with the security forces community manager supported the conclusion of the 1995 indefinite reenlistment study and revealed other concerns about the possibility of implementing indefinite reenlistment in the Navy. In particular, Navy staff cited the loss of a symbolic opportunity for personnel to renew their commitment to service at each reenlistment point, which is considered important to the Navy's culture of service. The opportunity for personnel to communicate with their Command Master Chief on a regular (and required) basis to air grievances and discuss their progress, strengths, and weaknesses is also perceived as very important, and Navy personnel interviewed asserted that doing away with that regularly scheduled opportunity at reenlistment would be a significant loss.

Navy representatives interviewed conjectured that indefinite reenlistment would probably yield some savings in administrative costs, but not much, and would likely have a positive effect on retention. However, the Navy is currently overmanned and is looking at ways to reduce manning by targeting specific jobs for reduction while continuing to increase manning in others. Navy representatives argued that the reenlistment point gives high-quality people in fields with stalled promotion opportunities the option to transfer to other fields for more rapid advancement (e.g., through the Lateral Conversion Bonus program). Without this option, the Navy is concerned that ambitious top performers will be unsatisfied with their opportunities for advancement and leave the service rather than remain stalled in the Navy. It does not appear that the Navy considered linking this opportunity to other career points, such as promotion points.

Marine Corps Consideration of Indefinite Reenlistment

In 1996 the Marine Corps considered the adoption of indefinite reenlistment. The 1996 Center for Naval Analysis (CNA) study on the topic cited a 1993 proposal to amend Title 10 of the United States Code to authorize senior enlisted personnel to sign up for either a ten-year service contract or indefinite service for the ten years until retirement eligibility.[7] For this reason, it considered indefinite reenlistment at ten years of service, noted historical opposition to such proposals by the Marine Corps, and advised against it for the late 1990s as well:

> While most enlisted Marines who make it into the 11th year of service will eventually retire from the Corps, about one-third will not. It is imperative that the Marine Corps maintain the ability to make reenlistment decisions for career Marines after the 10th year of service. (Quester, 1996, p. 1)

This memo reported that of the Marines who separated between the 10th and 19th years of service between 1989 and 1995, 16 percent were not recommended for reenlistment and 46 percent were not eligible because of failure to meet standards or other disqualifying situations. Thus, an indefinite reenlistment or reenlistment for years 10 through 20 was seen as likely to retain people who should be screened out through the reenlistment process during that time interval. The Sergeant Major of the Marine Corps noted in 1996 that separating a poor performer under a contract is an arduous process relative to denying a reenlistment request (Lee, 1996). In addition, he noted that indefinite reenlistment would preclude the review of a Marine's record at each reenlistment point, which is considered an important quality check for the force.

The CNA report noted that in addition to the quality control issue, the service should consider that career Marines would lose certain privileges if denied the reenlistment process late in their career:

---

[7] The CNA did not elaborate on the source or nature of the proposal. The Marine Corps provided us with the four-page analysis summary (Quester, 1996).

I believe it has been important to Marines and their families to "mark" the third and subsequent reenlistments. The reenlistment process also gives the Marine a chance to "negotiate" with his monitor that may be important in the "quality of life" area. Both proposals (indefinite commitment or 10-year reenlistments) would deny these career Marines these opportunities in the future. (Quester, 1996, p. 2)

Sergeant Major Alford McMichael also considered the issue during his term as Sergeant Major of the Marine Corps (1999–2003). The indefinite reenlistment policy option came to his attention when a group of NCOs requested that the Marine Corps consider it because they did not want to undergo the reenlistment process.

The CNA revisited an indefinite reenlistment option for the Marine Corps in 2000, but found that the situation for senior enlisted personnel had not changed significantly, and its recommendations remained the same:

Had [Marines separated between the 10th and 19th years of service] not come for review due to the reenlistment requirement, we would have had over 3,600 Marines of questionable value, restricting promotion and stifling opportunity for those of lesser rank. (Quester and Lee, 2000, p. 1)

The Marine Corps supplied us with a Military Police Division comment on the indefinite reenlistment option produced in 2000, shortly after the CNA update (MP Division, 2000). Its opposition to the policy was explained as follows:

- All of the Marine force management models and tools would have to be changed and would have to operate initially with unknown retention rates for senior personnel under indefinite reenlistment.
- Unlike the Army, which at the time only offered Selective Reenlistment Bonuses to two occupations for soldiers with 10 to 14 years of service (retained on fixed contracts as an exception to indefinite reenlistment), the Marine Corps offered these bonuses

to 86 different occupations for a total of $3.6 million. Indefinite reenlistment would call for the creation of a substitute program.

- Indefinite reenlistment eligibility that includes a rank requirement would result in differential treatment for Marines in jobs with faster promotion tempos than those in slower advancing fields.
- Without the reenlistment screening process, unit commanders would have to bear the burden of identifying the thousands of senior Marines who should not be retained and initiating and processing their separations. (MP Division, 2000)

After fully considering indefinite reenlistment, Sergeant Major McMichael rejected the policy for two reasons: it would fail to screen out people who would otherwise "clog up the system," and the reenlistment process motivates people to keep themselves fit and up to Marine standards. He argued that the reenlistment hurdle itself improves morale because senior enlisted Marines take pride in proving to themselves, their peers, and their subordinates that they still meet the standards required to be a Marine.

In 2004 the Marine Corps representative from personnel management interviewed for this RAND research reiterated the potential negative consequences of indefinite reenlistments cited by the Marine Corps in 1996 and 2000. These include the loss of reenlistment rates as an important projection tool in measuring manning levels, reenlistment ceremonies, opportunities to negotiate duty stations or assignments, and opportunities to sell back leave at the end of a term. Another potential negative consequence cited was the loss of regular and required reviews of personnel performance at each reenlistment point and the negative effect it might have on the quality of the force. Finally, due to changes already implemented in the administrative system used for reenlistment, the elimination of the reenlistment process after a certain point was not expected to yield significant savings.

Air Force Consideration of Indefinite Reenlistment

In 1996 and 1997, an Air Force "tiger team" was assembled to determine the feasibility of implementing indefinite reenlistment.[8] After months of study, the group advised against the policy. It noted that, on the positive side, indefinite reenlistment "may enhance [the] image of NCOs by recognizing their professionalism and offers them a 'lifetime commitment.'" Furthermore, indefinite reenlistment would decrease the administrative burden of reenlistment processing. The disadvantages cited by the Air Force resemble the Navy's objections, namely that indefinite status would allow enlisted personnel to leave the service more easily or be recruited by the civilian sector, which would make the airman assignment system significantly more difficult to manage. Similarly, because data on reenlistment rates would no longer be available for personnel under indefinite status, it would be difficult to gauge the effects of other personnel management policies and programs. The Air Force team also thought indefinite reenlistment would make separating poor performers more difficult. The team suggested that, from the perspective of enlisted personnel, the loss of the reenlistment ceremony would be significant, because that ceremony presents a unique opportunity for personnel to reaffirm their commitment to service and for the Air Force to reaffirm its commitment to the member. In addition, the opportunity to sell back leave would be lost, except at retirement. Moreover, the Air Force questioned how selective reenlistment bonuses, which it uses widely, would be distributed under an indefinite reenlistment program. For all of these reasons, the Air Force staff position was to reject indefinite reenlistment for the active-duty enlisted force.

One consideration raised uniquely by the Air Force was the timing of implementation. There was a sense that it would not be feasible to introduce such a program in the environment of high-tempo deploy-

---

[8] This information is based on an undated "Talking Paper on Proposal to Initiate Indefinite Reenlistments" that was given to us by the Air Force. The paper summarizes conclusions from an Air Force tiger team study conducted in 1996 and 1997. Neither our Air Force representative nor we were able to locate a report directly from the tiger team.

ment, outsourcing, and other personnel management changes that were taking place at the time under the Quadrennial Defense Review.

In an interview we conducted in February 2004 with a retention expert from the Air Force staff (the chief of the Air Force Accession and Retention Bonus programs), many of the disadvantages put forth by the Air Force's 1996 study of indefinite reenlistment were reiterated, including the potentially negative effect on the airman assignment system and the loss of reenlistment rate data as a planning tool. Also persistent was the concern that an important check on the quality of personnel would be lost if the reenlistment process were no longer in place. Our primary Air Force contact also reported that the Air Force no longer supported the notion that indefinite status would enhance professionalism or serve as a status symbol in the Air Force. The restriction on selling back leave until retirement was viewed as a disincentive, and the possible loss of selective reenlistment bonuses remained a concern up until the legislative changes that permitted them to be used as retention bonuses as well. Air Force analyses also disagreed that administrative savings would be realized, because the Air Force is currently implementing a new automated system for the reenlistment process. Finally, the Air Force representative relayed that the possible retention benefits of indefinite reenlistment are not needed in the current environment, in which the Air Force is overmanned, moving to shape the force with mandatory retraining in certain occupations, and offering to waive active-duty service dates for those who want to separate early. In sum, the Air Force's internal assessments of the possibility of an indefinite service program in 1996 and in 2004 found that there would be no real benefits of that service's adoption of the policy.

Summary of Service Objections to Indefinite Reenlistment

After considering the adoption of indefinite reenlistment, the Navy, Marine Corps, and Air Force all decided against implementation of the policy. It is important to note that each of the services considered a specific Army-like implementation of the policy rather than a design that might be better suited to their particular service needs. In sum, the Navy, Marine Corps, and Air Force have not implemented indefinite reenlistment programs primarily because of the following concerns:

NCO Perspectives:

- Granting indefinite status would not add to the prestige of senior enlisted personnel.
- Enlisted personnel would lose benefits and negotiating power currently associated with the reenlistment process.
- The loss of reenlistment bonuses would harm morale.
- There would be fewer reenlistment ceremonies, which are valued by many troops and their families.

Force Management:

- Indefinite reenlistment would make separating poor performers more difficult than at present.
- Such a program would make it too easy for high-quality people with labor market alternatives to leave.
- Eliminating reenlistment would have an adverse effect on force planning because an exact separation date would be unknown.
- Without a contract, people might choose to leave to avoid deployment or sea duty.
- The loss of reenlistment bonuses would harm retention.
- In cases in which the administrative system for reenlistment is already automated, cost savings would be negligible.

In the next two chapters we explore these general areas of concern and consider whether alternative forms of program implementation might mitigate these negative aspects and offer enough benefits to warrant reconsideration for adoption.

CHAPTER THREE

Indefinite Reenlistment and the Career NCO

As noted in the previous chapter, Congress officially authorized the use of indefinite contracts primarily as a reward for senior enlisted personnel. The intention was to enhance the prestige of the NCO corps by recognizing their career commitment and eliminating the inconvenience of reenlistment. Yet within the Department of Defense, only the Army has implemented this program. In this chapter we explore whether indefinite reenlistment has had or is likely to have an impact on prestige, first by discussing prestige factors identified by scholars and then by considering service members' perceptions of NCO prestige and indefinite reenlistment. Finally we examine service members' perspectives on what the Navy, Marine Corps, and Air Force have been concerned might be negative effects of indefinite reenlistment on senior NCOs.

Occupational Prestige

Since the early 1900s social scientists have conceptualized, measured, and refined the notion of occupational prestige, or status. "Occupational prestige" is standing or estimation in the eyes of people with a shared set of beliefs about the symbolic ranking of occupations in society. Researchers and policymakers care about prestige as a component of socioeconomic status, a critical component of analysis of social disparities, job satisfaction and the labor market, health and well-being, influence in the political and economic system, and just about every other dimension of social life.

A common approach to assessing occupational prestige has been to ask people to rank-order a list of occupations. Remarkably, prestige rankings are generally consistent across rankers throughout the society, over time, and across cultures, although some minor variations have been revealed (Treiman, 1977; Wegener, 1992; Zhou, 2005). This consistency has been understood to reflect differences in power and privilege in society associated with positions in the labor market (Treiman, 1977). Efforts to use objective indicators of prestige demonstrate that the majority of the variation in subjective prestige rankings can be explained by the education level and income associated with an occupation (Wegener, 1992; Miech, Eaton, and Liang, 2003; Zhou, 2005). Other factors thought to increase occupational prestige include training, autonomy, intellectual challenge, limited accessibility, control over resources, scientific or technical knowledge, and institution position (such as centrality to the key mission or placement at the top of an organization) (Zhou, 2005).

We now examine enlisted service members' perceptions of the effects of indefinite reenlistment on the prestige of the services' NCO corps. Based on the literature just reviewed, one would not expect to observe an effect of contract status on perceptions of prestige. However, most of the literature on occupational prestige focuses on the perceptions of individuals outside the communities being rated, and it is unclear whether the same factors underlie perceptions of prestige within a target community.

Enlisted Personnel's Views of Indefinite Reenlistment and NCO Prestige

We conducted 23 focus groups with enlisted personnel in the four services. We requested eight service members of diverse ranks, services, units, and occupations per focus group in order to maximize the range of opinions we might encounter. We also achieved some diversity in gender and race/ethnicity. The actual focus group sizes for each service are listed in Table 3.1.[1] Attendance of the Army focus groups was well below what we anticipated. Despite the low turnout, the near unanimity of some of the views of the 23 soldiers with whom we spoke, in concert with similar opinions expressed in focus groups in the other services, gave us a sense of issues of concern regarding the Army indefinite reenlistment program. Indeed, given the sampling strategy that was used to maximize the diversity of participants and the focus group facilitator strategies to elicit a variety of viewpoints, the level of agreement on most of the issues was striking.

Each focus group met for an average of one and a half to two hours. One of the purposes of the focus groups was to ascertain whether enlisted personnel believe indefinite reenlistment status has any influence on the prestige of NCOs. After exploring service members' decisions to enlist and reenlist and their service experiences thus far, we discussed the current Army indefinite reenlistment program. Our questions focused not only on the Army's current program design, but also on other possible designs, such as qualifying for the status earlier or later in the career. We asked about issues raised in earlier research by the Army, Navy, and Air Force and mentioned by our service contacts in manpower and personnel offices, such as whether the reenlistment process was perceived as a hassle and whether soldiers would miss the reenlistment ceremonies or the opportunities to sell back leave. Focus group participants offered their own suggestions of how to increase the status of NCOs.

The general consensus among focus group participants in all four services was that indefinite reenlistment does not and would not enhance the prestige of NCOs. Rather, they believed that factors such as competition, selectivity, responsibility, skills, benefits, income, and personal reputation were more significant than whether an NCO was on a fixed or indefinite contract status. The senior reenlistment process previously used in the Army and the current senior reenlistment processes in the Navy and Air Force were not viewed by our sample as cumbersome or

---

[1] To make comparisons across groups, Krueger and Casey (2000) suggest conducting at least three focus groups per group of subjects, which in the case of our study was determined by service and grade.

Table 3.1
Focus Group Size by Service and Seniority

	Army		Navy		Marine Corps		Air Force	
	Junior Enlisted Personnel (E-4–E-6)	Senior Enlisted Personnel (E-7–E-9)	Junior Enlisted Personnel (E-3–E-6)	Senior Enlisted Personnel (E-7–E-8)	Junior Enlisted Personnel (E-3–E-5)	Senior Enlisted Personnel (E-6–E-9)	Junior Enlisted Personnel (E-4–E-6)	Senior Enlisted Personnel (E-7–E-9)
Group 1	2	4	6	3	5	6	6	5
Group 2	3	6	7	7	8	7	7	8
Group 3	4, 4[a]	–	8	8	8	9	8	9
Total	13	10	21	18	21	22	21	22

[a] We assembled an additional focus group to compensate for low turnout in the earlier sessions.

demoralizing. In fact, the Marines asserted that just the opposite was true for their service: The elaborate reenlistment requirements are a screening process through which those who pass successfully gain prestige and continued legitimacy. There were some differences between services in the reasons cited in support of judgments about the effects of indefinite reenlistment on prestige. We summarize the views of focus group participants from each service in the following sections.

Army Participants: Indefinite Status Is Not a Factor in Perceptions of NCO Prestige

According to our focus group participants, the current indefinite status has no effect on the prestige of senior enlisted members. Most junior enlisted soldiers were unaware of the program, so they did not realize that the senior NCOs were working under a different enlistment status than they were. Because they did not know about the program, it was not a basis for holding those of their superiors in the program in higher esteem. After the difference was explained to them, we were told that respect among service members is based on rank and, more important, on behavior—not on occupation or enlistment status. As one soldier summarized, "They earn respect by doing their job. I don't care about indefinite status."

When senior enlisted personnel were asked if indefinite status increased their prestige, one said, "I don't see it." Another responded, "Not with pay the way it is—we'll never be compared to officers." In both of the senior enlisted focus groups, the NCOs asked the researcher to explain why anyone would think indefinite reenlistment status would be linked to prestige.

Focus group participants agreed that the reenlistment process used today for junior enlisted soldiers is not arduous, and senior NCOs noted that the reenlistment process under the previous fixed-term system had been no more arduous. They reported that no special career counseling occurs at reenlistment, no additional requirements must be met, and, as one senior NCO described the process, "I didn't mind spending five minutes raising my hand." Thus, the elimination of the reenlistment process is not seen either as relief from any particular burden or as a privilege or symbol of being accorded higher status.

When asked what they believe might actually improve NCO prestige, soldiers suggested that increased pay, benefits, or other bonuses directed toward senior enlisted personnel would make a difference. At this time, they pointed out, most of the bonuses (some in the tens of thousands of dollars) are given to people just for entering the Army rather than as a reward for those who have performed well, raised their level of education, and dedicated their lives to the Army for a decade or more. These arguments are consistent with social science research demonstrating the significance of education and income in evaluations of prestige. Competency pay, pay raises or bonuses targeting career NCOs, or programs facilitating degree attainment (such as eArmyU[2]) likely would have a greater effect on prestige than does the indefinite reenlistment program.

Air Force Participants: Implementing Indefinite Reenlistment Would Not Increase the Prestige of Career NCOs

Junior and senior enlisted airmen both serve under fixed-term contracts. Airmen in our focus groups agreed that giving senior enlisted personnel an indefinite reenlistment status similar to that of officers would not be valued as a reward or viewed as a sign of prestige among their colleagues. One junior NCO who is a linguist commented, "In my field, there's no prestige in being an officer." Another suggested that prestige is derived from individual behavior: "In the Air Force, prestige only comes from people you know and respect—people that know who you are and what you do. It doesn't come from rank or years of service." None of the junior or senior enlisted airmen in our focus groups saw a policy change to open-ended enlistments as enhancing NCO prestige.

Our focus group participants from the Air Force described the reenlistment process as easy. According to them, it consists of get-

---

[2] EArmyU is a distance learning program that gives soldiers the opportunity to earn certificates or licenses related to their MOS, a GED, an associate's, bachelor's, or master's degree through Web-based courses that can be taken even while soldiers are on deployment. Enrolled soldiers receive up to 100 percent funding for tuition, books, and course fees, as well as a personal laptop computer, an email account, and an Internet service provider account. For more about this program, go to http://www.earmyu.com/public/public_about-auao_more-about-auao.asp.

ting a "career job reservation" for a space in a career field, submitting paperwork, and obtaining approval by the commander. The commander takes performance evaluations into account in the reenlistment approval process, but those evaluations are not conducted specifically at the reenlistment point and would not be affected by an indefinite reenlistment program. Focus group participants perceived, however, that nearly all service members are allowed to reenlist.[3]

Navy Participants: Indefinite Reenlistment Would Not Increase the Already High Prestige of Chiefs

In the Navy, the transition from the E-6 to E-7 pay grade,[4] or to the "Chief" ranks, is significant and recognized as such by all Navy ranks. Promotion to Chief is neither swift nor automatic; hence, a great deal of pride accompanies the title. Junior enlisted sailors in our focus groups did not think having an enlistment status similar to that of officers would increase the respect given to senior NCOs. As one person explained, "Enlisted personnel and Chiefs don't want to be treated like officers. Indefinite reenlistment wouldn't change the respect that they get."

The Navy Chiefs we spoke with, each of whom had served between 14 and 19 years, were unanimous in their belief that an indefinite reenlistment program would add nothing to their status: "The Chiefs are already a separate, elite group. We already have brotherhood and prestige. We are a group of professionals, and we wear the same uniform as the officers." The Chiefs considered themselves the "backbone of the Navy," and across the board balked at any policy that might be pitched as elevating their status by matching their service to that of officers: "That'd almost be a step down for us!"

According to our focus group participants, reenlistment serves as a screening process, and a request to reenlist might be rejected for

---

[3] Personnel did speculate that with the downsizing of the force, obtaining approval to reenlist might become more difficult. For example, one focus group member commented, "People with even one unfavorable mark are now probably less likely to get the okay." Another projected, "They are going to start looking to see if you've been in trouble, if you've had any article 15s, letters of reprimand, etc."

[4] Corresponding ranks in the Navy are Petty Officer First Class and Chief Petty Officer.

several reasons, including domestic problems, significant debt, or poor performance. Junior enlisted sailors also asserted that people who do not progress through the ranks or get promoted in time are likely to be forced out of the service. Although the reenlistment process for sailors was portrayed as more complex than that described by soldiers, Navy personnel still described it as typically "just a paper shuffle—a one-week hassle at most." The enlisted leaders we interviewed did not see the process as degrading or burdensome.

Marine Corps Participants: Reenlistment Screening Contributes to High NCO Status

Like the focus group participants in the Navy and the Air Force, the enlisted Marines did not view treatment comparable to that of officers under indefinite reenlistment as prestigious. Most were adamant that there is an important reason for officers and enlisted members to be in distinct categories, and that enlisted Marines do not generally want to be like officers. One said: "I could be an officer, but I respect the work of the enlisted." The senior enlisted Marines in the three focus groups, whose time in service ranged from 12 to 29 years, agreed that the indefinite reenlistment program was unnecessary for enhancing NCO prestige. Based on their experience, they argued that it could even undermine the quality and prestige of the senior enlisted ranks.

The Marines argued that an indefinite reenlistment program would eliminate the competitive reenlistment process, which would allow people to remain if they only met the minimum requirements and thus would reduce the respect and quality of Marines. Unlike the Army focus group participants, who believed that even the lowest-quality NCOs would be able to reenlist, the Marines believe that their system is designed to retain only those who are dedicated enough to keep themselves up to service standards.

One Marine who had been in the service nearly 30 years explained: "By eliminating reenlistment, you lose a tool to hold Marines accountable: evaluations, fitness, commander signatures, appearance, rifle/weapons qualification—the motivation to continue to meet the standards." Another senior NCO with 22 years of experience made a similar case for the reenlistment process: "It makes you bring yourself up to speed, clean house. The hassle is minor compared to what we reap." The Marine Corps is unique among the services in having such rigorous reenlistment requirements for career NCOs.

One master sergeant asserted that the functions of the job themselves should be viewed as rewards: "Staff NCOs shouldn't have to be catered to in terms of morale. We're mentors, leaders, psychologists, sometimes fathers to these kids. Our morale has to stay high, because they feed off of us." Senior enlisted Marines saw themselves as the source of motivation and morale, not as consumers in need of it.

The Marines argued that yet another reason they do not have a problem with the prestige of their enlisted leaders is that even their junior leaders are given a higher level of responsibility than their counterparts in the other services: "The Army has a lieutenant or an E-8 or E-9 do what we let a staff sergeant do." In each focus group, senior enlisted Marines asserted an organizational leadership development strategy of pushing power down the ranks. With greater power and responsibility comes greater prestige.

Thus, senior enlisted Marines feel a strong sense of pride in having achieved rank and having been permitted to remain in the Marine Corps, and do not feel any need to increase the prestige of their senior members.

Indefinite Reenlistment and NCO Morale

The Navy, Marine Corps, and Air Force have all previously considered and rejected the indefinite reenlistment. Some of the arguments cited against the policy suggested that a change to indefinite reenlistment could have a negative effect on NCO morale. In particular, concerns were expressed about the loss of opportunities for service members to sell back unused leave, receive reenlistment bonuses, negotiate duty locations, and receive recognition for their continued commitment to their service. We review the perspectives of enlisted personnel on each of those issues in the following sections.

For Service Members, the Financial Consequences of Indefinite Reenlistment Are Negligible

At the end of an enlistment period, service members have an opportunity to sell back unused leave (receive cash for leave days). There was consensus among the personnel in our focus groups that selling back leave should generally be avoided if possible. Troops receive compensation for unused leave days only in the form of their base pay, not their housing allowance or other benefits, and they must pay taxes on the money they receive. Our interviewees explained that the only sensible reason to sell back leave is if one accrues over the maximum 60 days allowed and the only other choice is to lose the money that that time represents altogether. One said, "I have never sold back leave. If you're going to stay in, you might as well use those days unless you're at the 60-day cap." Navy personnel in our focus groups reported selling back leave more than those in the other services did, because sea duty caused them to exceed the maximum number of leave days they could accumulate. The Chiefs especially felt their opportunity to take leave was severely limited by their responsibilities, so they viewed the cash they receive from selling back leave as better than nothing. One Chief pointed out that selling back leave can be useful when someone needs a lump sum of cash, for example, for a down payment on a car. Those who must either sell back leave or lose it naturally prefer to sell it back when on a ship in a tax-free zone.

If there were compelling reasons for implementing an indefinite reenlistment program and the services wanted to retain the career NCOs' option to sell back leave, that opportunity could be linked to another milestone in the career, such as reaching the 15th year of service or achieving the rank of E-7.

Previous evaluations of indefinite reenlistment considered the effects of the loss of the selective reenlistment bonus (SRB) and concluded that service members would suffer from that loss. Members of our focus groups revealed that the concerns of previous evaluations were either overly pessimistic or out of date. Army and Navy personnel noted that senior enlisted personnel generally do not receive reenlistment bonuses, so they were not concerned about the elimination of SRBs. Senior NCO Marines were not inclined to discuss the issue of SRBs at all. Although senior airmen also have limited eligibility for SRBs, they were dismayed by the possibility that SRBs would be unavailable under indefinite reenlistment. Regardless, the argument that indefinite reenlistment should be rejected because of the loss of SRBs is now moot, because the Army has replaced SRBs with retention bonuses. Our findings suggest that continuing to offer the retention bonus would be an important part of an indefinite reenlistment program for members of eligible occupations, particularly if adopted by the Air Force.

NCOs Have Limited Opportunities to Negotiate Duty Locations, Even When on Fixed-Term Contracts

Junior enlisted personnel expressed concerns that indefinite reenlistment would restrict or eliminate opportunities to negotiate for preferred locations, training, and jobs. One junior enlisted soldier said, "I wouldn't look forward to indefinite reenlistment at ten years . . . that's ten years of options. What if there is somewhere you want to go or an MOS [military occupational specialty] you want to train for?" Several of the junior enlisted sailors anticipated that the reduction of bargaining power, paired with the loss of bonuses at later reenlistment points, would make careerists feel underappreciated.

One senior NCO confirmed the perceptions of junior enlisted service members: "When you go indefinite, you're at the mercy of the Army needs. In the past, it was more in your hands." Other Army senior NCOs, however, argued that before becoming eligible for indefinite reenlistment, they had already experienced a loss of bargaining power at successive reenlistment points, as fewer positions were available to NCOs. Senior enlisted soldiers also explained that they have less power to negotiate location as they achieve the senior ranks because the closer they are to retirement, the more willing they are to accept an undesirable assignment rather than leave the military and walk away from their retirement benefit. For military personnel with more than 10 years of service, retirement eligibility after 20 years of service is a strong incentive to reenlist, and it tends to outweigh other incentives, such as attractive job assignments or locations.

Senior NCOs in the services with fixed-term contracts also reported an inability to negotiate assignments and schooling in the last half of their careers. All of the Air Force senior enlisted focus group participants agreed that they, too, had no bargaining power for assignments during the reenlistment process. Marine participants echoed the same: "The further up you go, the less flexibility there is." Similarly, the retirement benefit, prestige, and privileges that accompany the rank of Navy Chief are the primary rewards and incentives at that stage: "[There's] no point in trying to use power at reenlistment to influence your next assignment." Sailors have bargaining power during earlier reenlistments, but "when you're at eighteen [years of service], you'll go anywhere. It's 95 percent certain you'll be sent to Japan." In sum, the potential loss of bargaining power under indefinite reenlistment feared by the younger members of our focus groups may be largely unfounded, because even under fixed-term contracts, NCOs' inclination to negotiate diminishes as they approach retirement.

Unlike Most Senior Soldiers, Sailors, and Airmen, Marines Would Lament the Loss of Reenlistment Ceremonies

Reenlistment ceremonies are special occasions during which friends, family, and coworkers can come together to celebrate a service member's record of service and renewed commitment. Critics of indefinite reenlistment argued that these ceremonies are rituals in which people gain a sense of the esteem in which they are held, and thus losing them could hurt morale. However, reenlistment ceremonies were not an issue of great importance to most of our focus group participants. Most participants were indifferent about the issue. Only a few senior soldiers said that they had exercised their option to make reenlistment a special event, and in most cases, they were junior enlisted personnel at the time.

Although some junior enlisted personnel in the Army choose to make reenlistment a special ceremony, most of the junior enlisted soldiers with whom we spoke did not consider the reenlistment ceremony an important event. Indeed, most members of our focus groups said they would not miss it: "Just give me a piece of paper and a pat on the back. Most people feel this way. It would just make it that much easier."

Senior NCOs expressed similar sentiments: "It's a formality more than anything else. You just raise your hand in the unit."

Soldiers do have the option to make the ceremony a special occasion if they so choose. One senior NCO was proud to tell us of his last reenlistment ceremony in a helicopter. Some soldiers, we were told, prefer to have the top general reenlist them so that they can receive the general's "coin."[5] For most soldiers, though, even early in their career, the reenlistment ceremony appears not to invoke any sense of ritual or rite of passage.

Like their counterparts in the Army, junior enlisted sailors and airmen did not seem to place a large amount of importance on reenlistment ceremonies. For example, we heard these comments: "They're two seconds long." "They're not important. It's like a cliché, just something you have to do." "[I] wouldn't want to make it a big deal anyway." "You get a handshake, congratulations, and a 'Get back to work.'" Most would rather just "get their money [SRB] and get back to work." However, some enlisted personnel did comment that a reenlistment ceremony can be individualized and that some service members choose to make the ceremony exciting. One Air Force participant said he had his ceremony on the wing of an F-15 fighter jet. Others said the last reenlistment ceremony before retirement might also be particularly special. According to most personnel, though, the best part of the process is that the person who reenlists, and sometimes the entire unit, is excused from work the day of the ceremony.

The Navy Chiefs who participated in our focus groups described the reenlistment point as "nice" because "the mess makes you a special cake," but none thought they would miss the event. Reenlistment ceremonies were described as more relevant for sailors early in their careers who might be contemplating alternative employment. The end of the enlistment contract was not considered a decisionmaking point for those who had achieved the rank of Chief, and thus choosing to

---

[5] A specific unit or command coin is sometimes presented as a reward for performance or as a token in ceremonies. These coins are collected by some soldiers and are frequently on display in the offices of military personnel, including high-ranking military officers and civilian defense workers.

reenlist was not noteworthy: "Our reenlistment is a moot issue. We give no second thought to reenlisting."

If an indefinite reenlistment program were adopted in services in addition to the Army, it does not appear that the morale of Navy or Air Force senior personnel would be affected by the loss of reenlistment ceremonies. However, senior Marines value reenlistment ceremonies, so the elimination of such ceremonies under indefinite reenlistment would be of concern to the Marine Corps. Marines told us that the reenlistment ceremony itself is not viewed as particularly important, but the act of reenlistment is considered significant. One junior enlisted Marine said, "I like reenlistment and what it is about. It's a pat on the shoulder for serving for four years. It is the Marine Corps saying, 'We appreciate what you do for us.'" Others said indefinite reenlistment would take away the "look-forward-to moments" from which many service members draw motivation and inspiration. The reenlistment ceremony was valued by senior NCOs as a reminder of their oath and renewed commitment to the corps. Some Marines make the reenlistment ceremony a major event, inviting the commanding officer or commanding general to reenlist them. Some ceremonies take place while Marines are underwater, at a memorial, on top of a mountain, jumping out of a plane, flying over a particular landmark, hanging from the side of a rappel tower, or in other special settings. Marines often invite family and friends to attend or to witness the occasion.

The Positive Side of Indefinite Reenlistment for NCOs: The Option to Separate

After soldiers gave us their opinion of the program under faulty understandings of its parameters—that indefinite reenlistment was equivalent to signing a contract to remain in the Army until retirement—we explained that senior NCOs retain the right to separate once other contractual obligations related to relocation, schooling, or deployment were met. Sailors and airmen agreed with soldiers that more frequent opportunities to separate under indefinite reenlistment would be a positive change, allowing those who do not want to be in the service to leave, rather than negatively affecting the unit. One soldier explained, "If you get an E-6 or E-7 who doesn't want to be there, it has a big effect on working relationships and the running of a platoon." In addition, indefinite reenlistment would allow service members to weigh more seriously employment options that arise in the civilian world, which the soldiers viewed as a benefit.

Some Marines in our focus groups cautioned that indefinite reenlistment could make it too easy to leave the service, which would be tempting when circumstances or conditions were difficult. Right now, contracts provide a single point in time when service members can decide whether to recommit to service based on the entirety of their four- or six-year term. One junior enlisted Marine said:

> Under indefinite reenlistment you would think about your enlistment decision every day, instead of every four years. . . . You have bad days and bad months, but things can get better, and you have to stay in and stick it out. I'm glad we don't have the option to get out and make a rash decision.

Consistent with the data on continuation rates, most senior enlisted personnel doubted that they would leave after 12 or 14 years of service. However, service members anticipated that repeated deployments to Iraq might cause some career NCOs to change course—to leave and give up retirement rather than serve multiple long-term tours in a combat zone. Thus, the pattern that held for the initial years of the Army program may change if negative aspects of deployment outweigh the lure of retirement benefits.

Conclusion

Army leaders and members of Congress instituted indefinite reenlistment as a reward for NCOs' commitment to service and anticipated that senior enlisted personnel would embrace the new policy. Policymakers intended to enhance NCOs' prestige by acknowledging formally that senior leaders are careerists, by eliminating periodic reenlistments and the associated paperwork, and by giving senior NCOs more flexibility to initiate separation from service prior to retirement.

Some degree of prestige is inherent simply in reaching the rank of staff sergeant and serving ten years in the Army. As longer terms in the Army come to mean multiple combat tours, prestige may grow in recognition of sacrifice and service to this core organizational mission. But indefinite reenlistment, as implemented by the Army, does not appear to have had an impact on the prestige of the NCO corps. Our research suggests that junior enlisted soldiers may have little if any knowledge of this NCO status and that there is some confusion among senior NCOs about the details of the program. If our findings hold for the population at large, many soldiers may be unaware that they have the option to leave the service under indefinite reenlistment.

Indefinite reenlistment is automatic and mandatory for everyone in the Army at the prescribed rank and length of service, regardless of performance, and as such is not perceived by the focus group participants in our study to confer any special status on career NCOs. Rather than viewing the program as a reward for service, many soldiers in our focus groups believed that few if any valued benefits accompany the transition to indefinite reenlistment, and they noted that some positive aspects of reenlistment are lost. Focus group participants were less concerned about losing opportunities to sell back leave than the services had projected, and their opinions varied as to whether they would be affected personally by the loss of selective reenlistment bonuses (this issue has no longer been problematic since retention bonuses were authorized). Most service members did not attach personal meaning or significance to the reenlistment ceremony, although some of the Marines were vocal about not wanting to lose the opportunity for a meaningful reenlistment experience. The one benefit to an indefinite reenlistment program from the NCO perspective might be greater flexibility for NCOs to separate prior to retirement, although most of the participants in our focus groups did not anticipate that they would ever want to do so.

The findings from this study's focus groups as previously summarized suggest that mandatory indefinite reenlistment is not an effective tool for enhancing NCO prestige or morale. It is not perceived as recognition for superior performance, nor is it interpreted as a symbol of extraordinary dedication to service. We found no evidence that moving to a policy of indefinite reenlistment in the Navy, Marine Corps, or Air Force would enhance the prestige of their senior enlisted personnel. Indeed, our findings suggest that indefinite reenlistment has not affected perceptions of the prestige of senior NCOs in the Army.

CHAPTER FOUR

Effects of Indefinite Reenlistment on Force Management

In this chapter we examine the effects of indefinite reenlistment on the Army's enlisted force management capability, describe the force management tools employed in each of the services that offer fixed-term contracts to senior enlisted personnel, and discuss possible effects of indefinite reenlistment on force management in those services.

Effects of Indefinite Reenlistment on Army Force Management

During early consideration of indefinite reenlistment, critics cited potential negative effects on force management, including the management of retention and separation and force planning. The Army representatives we interviewed explained that the transition was very smooth and said that the service is pleased with the policy from a force management perspective.

The Army did not expect implementation of indefinite reenlistment to affect retention rates. The program was designed so that soldiers become eligible at a point in their careers when almost all soldiers opt to stay until they complete 20 years of service. We conducted an analysis of Army continuation rates for soldiers on indefinite contracts, and the results support the argument that the transition from fixed contracts to indefinite reenlistment had no appreciable effect on retention. There were no significant differences between continuation rates before and after the policy change.

Our findings from focus groups with Army enlisted personnel further reinforced the notion that indefinite reenlistment was not a significant factor in decisions to remain in the service. Indefinite reenlistment was not cited by any focus group participants in discussions of their reasons for reenlisting. Rather, successful performance, rewarding work, and benefits were some of the reasons soldiers chose to stay in the Army. Several of the senior NCOs who reenlisted said they reenlisted for the third or fourth time because they were doing well in the organization and enjoying their work: "The unit is like a family. It's a good feeling. When I became an NCO, I enjoyed the challenge of influencing other people. I love my job. I love putting on my uniform and helping people change for the better." A few NCOs had watched peers leave the service only to return after major disappointments in the civilian sector. Their peers showed them the value of the job security and benefits of military service. One soldier was particularly grateful for the support the military had provided him in paying his young son's medical bills, which had reached hundreds of thousands of dollars.

As noted earlier, the Army indefinite reenlistment program was designed so that soldiers become eligible at a point in their careers when they are very unlikely to separate from the service before retirement. Thus, although the contracts are indefinite, force planners can anticipate retention rates quite reliably. Service contracts other than enlistment contracts are additional sources of data that can be used to predict retention rates. Those obligations are typically related to permanent change of station, promotion, and schooling. For example, a time remaining in service (TRS) obligation for school attendance can be up to 36 months. TRS requirements may also be incurred for special training or career development programs. Soldiers attending the U.S. Army Sergeants Major Course incur a 24-month TRS obligation. A soldier who is in indefinite status and enrolls in the eArmyU educational system that provides a laptop computer must assume a three-year-service-remaining requirement. Thus, although senior enlisted soldiers do not have defined enlistment contracts, they are bound by other service obligations.

As was also noted earlier, one argument cited in support of indefinite reenlistment was that it would eliminate costs associated with processing reenlistments of senior personnel. Since then, the Army has implemented a real-time automated system for reenlistment and reclassification (called RETAIN) that has replaced the old paper processing of reenlistments. Thus, even if indefinite reenlistments had not been introduced for senior enlisted personnel, automation would have reduced the costs associated with processing reenlistments.

One other motivation for implementing indefinite reenlistment was the anticipation of cost savings associated with the elimination of SRBs; however, as discussed earlier, reenlistment bonuses have since been replaced by retention bonuses for Army personnel on indefinite contracts.

Service Reenlistment Policies and the Force Management Context in 2004

Each of the remaining services upholds a traditional fixed contract system for all enlisted personnel. Reenlistment may be strictly pro forma for some, but competitive for others. Still, a contract binds service member and service for a fixed period, whether one is a new enlistee or has already served 15 years. The size and composition of the force is managed through mechanisms such as competition for reenlistment, reenlistment bonuses, and job reassignments.

In the Navy

Navy representatives we interviewed reported that the Navy was over-manned due both to stop-loss policies linked to operations in Iraq and to otherwise high retention. It therefore implemented policies and force-shaping programs to reduce the size of the force while retaining quality personnel with the right mix of job skills. For example, the Navy eliminated exceptions to the rules that it commonly employed during times when it had a need for a greater number of personnel, such as allowing enlisted personnel to extend their service beyond the limits allowed by the "up-or-out" policy through selective continuation.

The Navy also created a "Perform to Serve" program to reduce overfilled jobs but retain high-quality first-term sailors in those fields by allowing them to transfer to career fields with better opportunities for promotion. Through this program the Navy compares all sailors requesting reenlistment in a given rating (occupation) in terms of performance indicators such as commanders' endorsements for reenlistment and promotion. Based on how enlistees compare with their peers, they are allowed to reenlist in the same occupation, transfer to an undermanned field, or leave the service.

During this study another career option introduced at the end of an enlistment term emerged: Operation Blue to Green,[1] This force-shaping program allows "blue" (Navy and Air Force) service members to laterally transfer into the "green" Army, which is actively seeking new recruits. Those who transfer may qualify for bonuses if they enter undermanned Army occupations.

Selective reenlistment bonuses are the only service-level retention tool, but a Navy representative reported that many of the individual commands also have incentive packages for reenlistment. Those incentives may take the form of books of coupons (which may include a 10 percent discount on Exchange purchases), 24 hours of paid leave, and reserved parking spaces. For higher-ranking enlisted personnel looking for a change of pace or additional bonuses, a lateral conversion bonus is available for those willing to cross-train for undermanned fields, such as security forces.

The Navy's reenlistment process was recently automated, so the administrative burden associated with processing reenlistments has been reduced. One incentive available at reenlistment is that a sailor may be able to negotiate for schooling, training opportunities, or duty stations in exchange for a certain reenlistment period.

In the Air Force

In fiscal year 2004, the Air Force also needed to reduce its force; it found it had about 16,600 more personnel than it had projected due to high retention and reenlistment rates. The service intended for enlisted

---

[1]   Information available at www.goarmy.com/btg/.

personnel to constitute 12,700 of the personnel cuts (HQ AFPC, n.d.). Thus, the Selective Reenlistment Program employed a number of force-shaping tools: restricting extensions to the "up-or-out" policy, allowing voluntary transfer to the reserves, shortening service commitments, rolling back separation dates for airmen with 14 years of service or less, and facilitating transfers of existing airmen to undermanned jobs rather than enticing new people through bonuses (Jumper, 2004).

Reenlistment is now more competitive than it had been. First-term airmen must now be selected by their commander for reenlistment and must submit a career job reservation (CJR). The CJR program was adopted to prevent surpluses in some occupations and shortages in others. Some fields are constrained, and first-term airmen must compete with other airmen applying to reenlist in the same occupation. Enlistees in undermanned fields can have greater confidence that they will be allowed to reenlist in their current occupation rather than having to retrain for another occupation or leave. Airmen requesting reenlistment may also request to be retrained for another career field or even to transfer to the Army through the previously mentioned Operation Blue to Green. Members who are not deemed eligible by their command or do not submit a CJR must leave the service at the end of their enlistment contract. Second-term and career airmen must also obtain a commander's recommendation for reenlistment. If not recommended for reenlistment, troops can appeal the decision, but in general the Air Force gives the reenlistment decisionmaking power to the unit commanders.

In the Marine Corps

At the time of this study, the demand for ground forces to serve in Iraq and Afghanistan was high. The Marine Corps, already a significantly smaller service than its counterparts, stood in contrast to the Navy and Air Force in this period in that it was not seeking to downsize its force. On the other hand, it was not facing the same recruiting challenges of the Army. So the Marine Corps at this time was seeking neither to tighten screening mechanisms to reduce personnel from its ranks nor to loosen its entry, reenlistment, or promotion standards to attract or retain a greater number of Marines.

The Marine Personnel Management Division attributes a number of recent developments in how it manages its career force to a retention crisis in 2000. At that time, the size of the career force (which comprises Marines in their second and subsequent terms) had been in steady decline and had reached an all-time low, decreasing from 39.5 percent of the force in 1988 to 30.3 percent in 2000. One of the changes was to authorize a lump-sum payment of selected reenlistment bonuses in fiscal year 2001 (FY01), which contrasts with other service practices of providing part of the bonus up front and the remainder later in the enlistment contract. An even more dramatic change was the redistribution of the SRBs. In FY01 almost all SRBs were offered during first-term reenlistments; in FY02, 40 percent of bonuses went to the career force. Offering SRBs to members of the career force resulted in significantly higher continuation rates for Marines with 9 to 14 years of service.[2]

Today, management of all military Marine Corps personnel—enlisted and officer, active and reserve, as well as retirees—is conducted through a single integrated computer program and database known as the Marine Corps Total Force System.[3] This system allows manpower planners to match personnel requirements with personnel "inventory" and to adjust recruitment and reenlistment plans to meet the goals of the service.

At the end of their first enlistment contract, Marines are matched with available positions. This process is referred to as First-Term Alignment, and it is a competitive process for those in highly desired occupations. Reenlistment for Marines in those fields is not guaranteed, even for those who perform well. For all first-term Marines, the opportunity to reenlist begins in October and closes by July. At the beginning of the cycle, Marines may request to reenlist in their military occupational

---

[2]   https://lnweb1.manpower.usmc.mil/manpower/mi/mra_ofct.nsf/mmea/Career+Counsel ing+and+Evaluation+Unit+-+Retention. The Marine officer who manages first-term realign-ment informed us that the Marine Corps relies upon continuation rates to assemble its force management plans.

[3]   The system is specified in a memo designated "MCTFSPRIUM 19OCT04," available at http://64.233.161.104/search?q=cache:3RH7mO9YKz4J:www.missa.manpower.usmc.mil/ prim.asp%3Fc%3D1+%22total+force+retention+system%22&hl=en&ie=UTF-8.

specialty (MOS). Every reenlistment package requires a commander's signature endorsing the reenlistment. In cases in which a commander is not confident about endorsing reenlistment, probationary reenlistment can be recommended.

Positions open to Marines reenlisting for the first time are generally filled through sequential processing, which means Marines in highly desired career fields must prepare and submit their reenlistment requests as quickly as possible. High-quality applicants who do not submit their reenlistment packages early may not find an open position in their MOS. In such a case, a Marine's only options are to leave the service or to laterally transfer to an MOS with a personnel shortage. At the time of the first reenlistment, about 14 percent of Marines change their MOS, either by personal choice or to remain in the service.[4] To address concerns about the practice of selecting the first to apply over the best to apply, a new system for competitive fields, known as fast filling military occupational specialties (FFMs), was piloted in June 2003. Now an FFM board reviews reenlistment requests in those highly desired fields and selects only the top Marines for reenlistment (Agg, n.d.). Other fields are still filled on a first-come basis.

Subsequent Term Realignment refers to the matching of Marines reenlisting after their second or subsequent term with open job assignments. MOS availability does not prohibit the reenlistment of second-term Marines. Special effort is devoted to finding positions for career Marines, because the culture of the service dictates that occupations are secondary to institutional identity. This practice stems from the view that "every career force reenlistment must be viewed in the context of properly distributing a scarce and valuable resource" (Manpower and Reserve Affairs Department, 2001, p. 19). In January 2005, former Sergeant Major of the Marine Corps Alford McMichael explained it to us this way: "Leadership is valued over skills. I'd rather have a strong leader and a weak cook than a weak leader and a strong cook." Thus, the organization has developed a strategy to find a place for its top Marines, regardless of occupation.

---

[4] This information was provided to us by a Marine Corps officer in personnel management who runs the models for the First-Term Alignment Program.

Likely Effects of Indefinite Reenlistment on Force Management in the Navy, Marine Corps, and Air Force

The overview of current force management in the Navy, Marine Corps, and Air Force reveals a number of tools designed to help the services achieve the right size, quality, experience, and skill mix among their enlisted forces. Next we consider the likely effects of indefinite reenlistment force management in those services.

Recruiting

It is unlikely that 18- to 25-year-olds would be motivated to join the services based on the length of their employment contract some ten years down the line. We know of no research on the motivations for enlistment that indicates that latter career term details are even thought about at such an early career stage. Typically youth report joining for educational benefits, job training, travel, the opportunity to leave their hometown, personal challenges and growth, patriotism, pay and benefits, and job security (see, for example, Asch, Du, and Schonlau, 2004; Buddin, 2005; Appendix B).[5] Furthermore, we are unaware of any Army recruiting materials that mention indefinite reenlistment in the second half of the career as a feature in marketing itself to today's youth. Even in the foreign military examples of indefinite reenlistment we reviewed, most people join for an initial fixed term. This entry stage serves as a trial period for determining whether the service is right for the individual and vice versa. Career terms come into play in most cases only for those entering a second or subsequent term of enlistment.

Retention and Separation

Repeatedly we heard in focus groups in each of the services that for personnel with more than 10 years of service, the 20-year retirement was an irresistible incentive to "stick it out," even for those less satisfied with their careers than are others or ineligible for reenlistment bonuses.

---

[5]   Soldiers conducting a Web search for the topic may encounter this message at http://members.tripod.com/thereupman/id33.htm or at http://usmilitary.about.com/library/mil-info/blarmyreenlist.htm.

Junior enlisted soldiers shared similar sentiments about the impact of indefinite reenlistment on their decisionmaking process: "Indefinite status doesn't matter to me. If I am staying in that long anyway, I would stay regardless of the program." Nobody in any of the focus groups thought that the indefinite reenlistment status had made or would make them any more or less likely to reenlist. Data from our focus groups with Navy, Marine Corps, and Air Force personnel suggest that similar effects of indefinite reenlistment (or a lack thereof) on retention could be expected in the other services.

Cost of Reenlistment Bonuses Versus Retention Bonuses

The 1992 Army study predicted that bonus savings would accompany the end of reenlistment for senior enlisted personnel due to the elimination of SRBs. A sergeant first class in one of our focus groups who was in the service at the time indefinite reenlistment was implemented recalled, "My first thought was that they wanted to save money on bonuses." However, Zone C reenlistment bonuses (for 10 to 14 years of service) have not been applied in the Army since January 31, 1986.[6]

The Army has been able to contain its SRB growth relative to the other services. A November 2003 U.S. General Accounting Office assessment of the SRB programs of the services shows an Army budget in 2003 at $101 million, up from $67 million in 1997 (prior to indefinite reenlistment), which is a multiple of 1.5. In comparison, the Navy budget multiplied by 1.85, from $188 million in 1997 to $348 million in 2003, and the Marine Corps SRB budget more than tripled, from $20 million to $62 million. The Air Force has become most dependent on reenlistment bonuses: Its total SRB budget grew from $34 million in 1997 to $223 million in 2003, increasing by a multiple of roughly 6.5, with airmen with over 70 percent of the various skills eligible for such a bonus.[7] In comparison with the SRB increases in the other services, the Army's increase was relatively limited. However, we are not able to determine whether the difference can be attributed to the implementation of indefinite reenlistment.

---

[6]   See http://www.hrc.army.mil/site/active/epret/srb.htm.

[7]   The source for the latter number is Asch et al., 2002, p. xviii.

Although the possibility of reenlistment bonuses disappeared for senior enlisted personnel under indefinite reenlistment, other policy changes now make bonuses available to soldiers under indefinite reenlistment. Section 633 of the National Defense Authorization Act (NDAA) for 2001 authorized retention bonuses for people with critical skills who were willing to extend their service obligations by one year, and Section 621 of the 2005 NDAA specifically revised the language to note that soldiers under indefinite reenlistment qualify for such bonuses. Thus, a bonus eliminated in one form (reenlistment) has reappeared in a similar form, but with a different name (retention bonus).

Force Planning

One of the concerns, particularly of the Air Force planners we spoke with, was that the elimination of reenlistment contracts for senior NCOs would also eliminate their ability to predict who would stay and what new personnel they needed to enlist and train.

But what would be the cost of switching from a system that tracks enlistment contracts to one that tracks other types of service contracts? The Air Force maintains a Military Personnel Data System that is a live, ever-changing database that it can and does use for force management and planning. RAND has access to the monthly snapshots of those files, the Active Officer Extract File, and, for enlisted personnel, the Active Airmen Extract File. Those file layouts show that active duty service commitments are recorded for both officers and enlisted personnel. The officer file allows up to six commitment dates and possible reasons for those commitments (pilot training, USAF Academy or ROTC obligations, etc.) to be recorded. For enlisted personnel, three spaces are provided for the same information: dates and reasons, such as moves to another base, that service obligations may be incurred. So if the Air Force could no longer rely on the end of four-year reenlistment contracts to predict possible losses, it already has the resources to calculate those dates based on other service commitments. The primary difference we can see is that those service commitments are generally, if not always, shorter than four years; a commitment following a move, for example, is two years. However, as we have stated elsewhere, for all services personnel retention near the end of the 20-year career is consistently extremely high (over 90 percent for those who fall under the Army's indefinite reenlistment criteria). Thus, no new databases or costly changes to existing databases would need to be made in order to adjust planning from enlistment contracts to other service obligation contracts.

Job Security for NCOs or a Cost-Saving Downsizing Option for the Services?

Following the end of the Cold War, the services, the Army in particular, relied on a number of programs to dramatically downsize their forces. From January 1992 to October 1995 a temporary Department of Defense (DoD) program offered sizable financial incentives to certain midcareer personnel to voluntarily leave the military; those funds were paid out either over a period of time, as a voluntary separation incentive, or as a single lump sum special separation benefit (Asch and Warner 2001). As another downsizing tool in 1992, Congress also authorized the services to offer military retirement at 15 years of service. Further personnel cuts in the form of involuntary separations and early retirements without any special accompanying pay were accomplished through RIFs (reductions in force) and SERBs (selective early retirement boards).

Thus, in 1998, when the U.S. Army decided to pursue a policy of indefinite reenlistment, its members had just survived severe personnel cuts, including involuntary separations. Army leaders and members of Congress instituted indefinite reenlistment as a reward for NCOs' commitment to service, and they anticipated that senior enlisted personnel would embrace the new policy as a form of job security. Policymakers also intended the change to acknowledge formally that senior leaders are careerists by eliminating periodic reenlistments and the associated paperwork and by giving such career soldiers more flexibility to initiate separation from service prior to retirement.

In 2004 Army job security was not a concern for most soldiers, whether under indefinite reenlistment or not. Barring major misconduct or criminal behavior, soldiers in our focus groups were confident that the Army's demand for personnel to sustain operations in Iraq and Afghanistan guaranteed them ongoing employment. Indeed, some troops feared that instead they will not be able to retire or separate when they choose to because of deployment needs and stop-loss policies. In this era, senior NCOs place little value on affirmations of job security. Indeed, one skeptical senior NCO asserted, "The Army sold this as something that would improve morale. But the reason they did it was security for themselves. From then on a career soldier who wanted out would have to ask."

Given that the Navy and the Air Force are downsizing, as was the Army in 1998, one might expect enlisted personnel in those services to view indefinite reenlistment in the same light Army leaders and Congress did nearly a decade ago. Yet Navy and Air Force participants in our focus groups did not welcome indefinite reenlistment as a source of job security; instead, they interpreted the term "indefinite" to suggest that they might be easy targets for personnel cuts. They reported a sense of security in a fixed contract, which they believed guaranteed them a job for a set number of years despite their service's need to downsize or reshape the enlisted force.

Indeed, the elimination of fixed-term contracts under indefinite reenlistment and the demand for soldiers at the time of the study may explain why several of our Army focus group participants wondered if the new program was aimed at providing the service greater security to retain senior enlisted personnel. For example, one Army NCO stated, "I don't see anything detrimental about it, but there's nothing beneficial either. Except for the Army—they've got you [committed] with that one." Expressing a similar view, one first sergeant said that indefinite reenlistment "doesn't do anything but make it more certain for the Army. This is more for the Army, not for the soldier." Another senior NCO gave his interpretation of the policy change: "They lost a lot of senior NCO experience after the [Gulf] War. This was just a way to keep NCOs in. I think that's why it was implemented." So the policy change, rather than producing a "peace of mind" or job security for this group, was interpreted as providing greater security for the Army by providing more continuous service of NCOs. (This attitude was based on their misperception that they were obligated to serve until retirement or they reached their RCP.)

Saving Retirement Costs by Increasing Opportunities for Late-Career Voluntary Separation

As we noted in the previous chapter, the single feature that service members found attractive about indefinite reenlistment was the notion that they would have more frequent opportunities to choose to leave the service, although none of them thought they would, due to the great pull of the retirement benefit. In a period of downsizing, if enough people take advantage of the greater number of opportunities to leave under indefinite reenlistment, the services could save funds in separation incentive pay and retirement pay. However, this increased opportunity to separate could be a liability when the services need to retain senior NCOs. For example, it is possible that the frequency of deployment and the generous salaries offered by private contractors could erode individuals' personal evaluation of the worth of the retirement benefit and cause them to take advantage of their increased number of opportunities to separate. If retaining senior enlisted were key, the policy might cost more in this case because the Army might need to offer retention bonuses.

Cost Savings When Involuntary Separations Are Necessary

Although the Army's indefinite reenlistment documents never suggest that the service would involuntarily separate NCOs serving under the program, the possibility might be entertained in the event another drawdown were needed or if retention among the senior ranks and/or in particular specialties were too high. In fact, two of the uniformed services, the Navy and the Air Force, were beginning to reduce the size of their forces at the time of this study.

If the Navy and Air Force had indefinite reenlistment programs, they would have greater flexibility to separate senior enlisted personnel than is allowed by reenlistment windows, and they would not have to offer separation incentive pay. Currently the law protects service members with between 18 and 20 years of service from being involuntarily separated and thus losing their retirement benefit,[8] and the Air Force

---

8   U.S. Title 10, Subtitle A, Part II, Chapter 59, §1176. For enlisted members, there is retention after completion of 18 or more years of service, but fewer than 20.

offers extra protection for airmen with 16 years of service ("Administrative Separation of Airmen," Air Force Instruction 36-3208). Such job security and the prospect of retirement pay after 20 years are a significant benefit of military service, and to take that away might have a broader negative impact than the organization would be willing to sustain.

Obviously, involuntary separations offer financial savings, but not without other costs associated with such policies, such as reduced morale, performance, and organizational commitment among service members who survive downsizing (McCormick, 1998; Thornhill and Saunders, 1998). Focus group findings from our study support the likelihood of a negative reaction to an indefinite reenlistment program in which the service retained the right to separate career soldiers for force management purposes.

Air Force senior NCOs appreciated enlistment contracts as providing them a guaranteed job until the end of the contract, which was not inherent to the open-ended status of officers. One Chief Master Sergeant who had served over 27 years reported: [I've] "seen three officer RIFs since I've been in. They ask for volunteers; if they don't get it, it's involuntary." A Master Sergeant responded: "I'd be concerned about getting 'RIFed' [under indefinite reenlistment]. One reason I re-signed [reenlisted] was that I know the economy is bad, and I know that I have a job for four years."

The contract was also seen as beneficial for "holding people past the bad days." With a contract in hand, airmen were confident that if they make a mistake, have a personality clash with a leader, or let their work suffer due to personal problems such as a divorce, they cannot be fired instantly and will have a chance to recover or make up for their mistakes. So contracts were seen as more secure than indefinite status.

The focus group participants said that the Air Force had recently announced it would eliminate 16,000 positions, and they hoped that after volunteers, less desirable airmen would be separated. Others were worried about the lack of a contract under indefinite reenlistment and the ability such a plan would give the Air Force to invoke a stop-loss policy for long periods of time or to separate someone at 19 years of service, just before retirement eligibility.[9]

At the time we conducted our focus groups, the Navy not only was beginning to cut its personnel strength but was increasing its rate of deployments and decreasing the time between them. One Chief we interviewed thought that the only advantage of an indefinite reenlistment program would be job security unless the Navy reserved the right to separate people under this status: "Under downsizing, I'd be worried that this would be an easy way to get rid of people, and then we'd lose out on our retirement." The junior enlisted personnel also worried that an open-ended enlistment would "allow the military to get rid of you right before your retirement." Indefinite reenlistment was questioned as possibly "a way for the Navy to get people out of the Navy and just save some money."

The case of the Marine Corps highlights an interesting tradeoff: One of the reasons Marines argued that their senior enlisted personnel excel and command such prestige is that reenlistment is not a right or a guarantee, but something they view as having to be achieved.

---

[9] As noted earlier, legislation prohibits involuntary separation so close to retirement.

CHAPTER FIVE

Conclusions and Recommendations

When the Army designed its indefinite reenlistment program, no negative impact on force planning was expected because eligibility for indefinite reenlistment was set to pair with consistently high retention rates. That expectation was confirmed. There seems to have been no change in the Army's ability to do force planning since it introduced indefinite reenlistment. It is therefore reasonable to expect that if the other services were to choose eligibility criteria so that the lure of retirement would virtually guarantee continued service from everyone under indefinite reenlistment, their force planning capabilities also would be unaffected. Switching to a policy of indefinite reenlistment or eliminating such a policy would have no appreciable effect on this outcome of interest.

There is also little compelling evidence that such a policy would save significant amounts of funding. Even without automation of the reenlistment process, there is no clear indication that significant savings would appear. Retention bonuses have replaced reenlistment bonuses, which at least in the Army were not offered at the affected level of seniority anyway. Funds could be saved if this policy were implemented to allow the services to initiate involuntary separations, but the likely organizational costs in morale, productivity, and commitment make this alternative extremely unattractive. From a force management and cost perspective, we see no real benefit to warrant either changing from a fixed contract to an indefinite program or vice versa.

Should reforms to the retirement system be adopted so that the military career was significantly lengthened, it might be worthwhile to consider a European-style hybrid of limited-term and career-tracked service members, although it is not clear whether Americans would welcome further stratification within the current structure. Still, such a mix could serve to motivate and reward the top performers with career status, and the fixed-term pool could be the labor force that would be expanded and contracted to meet shifting demands without having to "buy out" many career NCOs during downsizing.

For the current enlistment structure, however, our research found no evidence that the potential benefits of converting to indefinite reenlistment outweigh the risks for the Navy, Marine Corps, and Air Force. Thus, we recommend that they continue their current fixed-contract programs for senior enlisted personnel. However, there is no evidence that the Army's indefinite reenlistment program is producing any degree of harm that warrants a reversion to fixed contracts; thus, we also recommend the status quo for the Army's senior reenlistment policy.

Army Policy Message on the Indefinite Reenlistment Program[1]

POLICY MESSAGE 98-19   18 AUGUST 1998

1. THIS IS A RETRANSMISSION OF DA [Department of the Army] MESSAGE DTG R 131810Z AUG 98.

*************BEGINNING OF RETRANSMISSION***********

RTTUZYUW RUEADWD7722 2251517-UUUU—RUERCOL.

ZNR UUUUU ZYW ZOC ZEO T ALL US ARMY REPS AND ACTIVITIES

R 131810Z AUG 98

FM DA WASHINGTON DC//DAPE-MPE//

TO ALARACT

BT

UNCLAS ALARACT 086/98 SECTION 01 OF 02

SUBJECT: IMPLEMENTATION OF THE INDEFINITE REEN-LISTMENT PROGRAM AR 601-280 (ARMY RETENTION PROGRAM) AND CHANGES TO AR 635-200 (ENLISTED SEPARATION)

---

[1] Memo provided to us by the Army G-1 (Office of the Deputy Chief of Staff for Personnel).

1. THE FOLLOWING CHANGES TO AR 601-280 WILL BE EFFECTIVE 1 OCTOBER 1998: REGULAR ARMY [RA] CAREER SOLDIERS IN THE RANK OF STAFF SERGEANT OR HIGHER WITH MORE THAN 10 YEARS OF ACTIVE FEDERAL SERVICE (AFS) WILL BE REQUIRED TO REENLIST FOR AN "UNSPECIFIED" TERM OF SERVICE UPON REENLISTMENT. AFFECTED SOLDIERS MUST HAVE OVER 10 YEARS AFS ON THE DATE OF REENLISTMENT TO BE ELIGIBLE FOR THE PROGRAM. SOLDIERS WITH 10 YEARS OR LESS AFS ON THE DATE OF REENLISTMENT WILL STILL REENLIST FOR A SPECIFIED TERM UNDER EXISTING POLICIES.

2. POLICY GOVERNING THE INDEFINITE REENLISTMENT PROGRAM WILL BE CONTAINED IN FORTHCOMING REVISED AR 601-280 (ARMY RETENTION PROGRAM). PARAGRAPH 3-16 (INDEFINITE REENLISTMENT PROGRAM) IS ADDED TO AR 601-280 AS FOLLOWS:

A. THE SECRETARY OF THE ARMY MAY ACCEPT REENLISTMENTS FROM REGULAR ARMY SOLDIERS FOR AN UNSPECIFIED OR INDEFINITE TERM OF SERVICE IAW 10 USC, 505(D). ALL RA ENLISTED SOLDIERS WITH OVER 10 YEARS ACTIVE FEDERAL SERVICE ARE REQUIRED TO REENLIST FOR AN INDEFINITE TERM UNLESS OTHERWISE EXEMPTED ELSEWHERE IN THIS REGULATION.

B. ELIGIBILITY. RA SOLDIERS IN THE RANK OF SSG-CSM WHO ARE ELIGIBLE FOR REENLISTMENT IAW CHAPTER 3, THIS

REGULATION, TO INCLUDE THOSE WITH APPROVED WAIVERS, AND HAVE MORE THAN 10 YEARS AFS ON THE DATE OF REENLISTMENT WILL BE REQUIRED TO REENLIST FOR AN UNSPECIFIED PERIOD OF TIME. SOLDIERS WITH A SERVICE REMAINING REQUIREMENT WILL ONLY BE ALLOWED TO REENLIST, NOT EXTEND IF THEY HAVE OVER 10 YEARS AFS, EXCEPT FOR HUMANITARIAN REASONS OR PENDING OTHER PERSONNEL ACTIONS.

C. CONSIDERATIONS. SOLDIERS ON INDEFINITE STATUS MUST RETIRE UPON REACHING THE APPLICABLE RETENTION CONTROL POINT [RCP] FOR THEIR RANK. IF PROMOTED, THE SOLDIER IS THEN PERMITTED TO SERVE TO THE RCP FOR THEIR NEW RANK. SOLDIERS WILL NOT BE ALLOWED TO EXCEED THE RCP BY MORE THAN 29 DAYS.

D. VOLUNTARY SEPARATION REQUESTS. SOLDIERS ON INDEFINITE STATUS MAY REQUEST VOLUNTARY SEPARATION IAW AR 635-200 (SEE PARAGRAPH 4, BELOW) PROVIDED THEY HAVE MET SERVICE REMAINING REQUIREMENTS AS DIRECTED BY HQDA [Headquarters, Department of the Army]. SOLDIERS WHO DESIRE TO SEPARATE IN LIEU OF COMPLYING WITH ASSIGNMENT INSTRUCTIONS, MUST REQUEST SEPARATION WITHIN 30 DAYS OF NOTIFICATION OF ASSIGNMENT INSTRUCTIONS. UPON DA APPROVAL, THESE SOLDIERS WILL BE SEPARATED WITHIN SIX MONTHS UNLESS SERVING ON OVERSEAS OR RESTRICTED TOUR. SOLDIERS ON OVERSEAS OR RESTRICTED TOUR WILL BE SEPARATED WITHIN SIX MONTHS OF NORMAL TOUR COMPLETION DATE.

E. REDUCTION IN RANK AND REMOVAL FROM PROMOTION LIST. SOLDIERS WHO EXCEED RCP AS A RESULT OF REDUCTION OR REMOVAL FROM A PROMOTION LIST WILL BE PROCESSED IAW PARAGRAPH 3-8G AND TABLE 3-1 THIS REGULATION. SOLDIERS WHO HAVE ATTAINED 18 YEARS AFS WILL BE PERMITTED TO RETIRE ON THE FIRST DAY OF THE MONTH FOLLOWING THE MONTH THEY REACH 20 YEARS AFS, UNLESS SEPARATED EARLIER UNDER APPLICABLE ADMINISTRATIVE, PHYSICAL DISABILITY, OR UCMJ [Uniform Code of Military Justice] PROVISIONS.

3. PARAGRAPH 3-8G(2) AND TABLE 3-1 TO AR 601-280 ARE CHANGED AS FOLLOWS:

G. RANK (NON-WAIVABLE).

(2) EXCEPT FOR SOLDIERS SERVING INDEFINITE REENLIST- MENTS, SOLDIERS WHO REACH THEIR RCP DURING THEIR CURRENT ENLISTMENT AGREEMENT, EITHER THROUGH LENGTH OF SERVICE, REDUCTION IN RANK, OR BY REMOVAL FROM A PROMOTION LIST, WHETHER VOLUNTARY OR INVOLUNTARY, MAY SERVE UNTIL CON- TRACTED EXPIRATION TERM OF SERVICE (ETS), UNLESS THEY ARE SEPARATED EARLIER UNDER APPLICABLE ADMINISTRATIVE, PHYSICAL DISABILITY, OR UCMJ SEPARATION PROVISIONS. SOL- DIERS IN THIS CATEGORY WHO ARE ELIGIBLE MAY APPLY FOR RETIREMENT. SOLDIERS WITH LESS THAN 18 YEARS AFS SERVING INDEFINITE REENLISTMENTS WHO EXCEED RCP AS THE RESULT OF A REDUCTION IN RANK MAY SERVE TO MINIMUM RETIREMENT

ELIGIBILITY UNLESS THEY ARE SEPARATED EARLIER UNDER
APPLICABLE ADMINISTRATIVE, PHYSICAL DISABILITY, OR UCMJ
SEPARATION PROVISIONS.

TABLE 3-1

RETENTION CONTROL POINTS

RANK	TOTAL ACTIVE SERVICE IN YEARS
PVT-PFC	3
CPL/SPC	10
CPL/SPC (PROMOTABLE)	10
SGT	15
SGT (PROMOTABLE)	15
SSG	20
SSG (PROMOTABLE)	22
SFC	22
SFC (PROMOTABLE)	24
1SG/MSG	24
1SG/MSG (PROMOTABLE)	30
CSM/SGM	30

NOTES

(1) THE RCP FOR SOLDIERS IN THE RANKS OF SSG(P)
AND ABOVE WHO ARE ASSIGNED TO SPECIAL BANDS (WEST POINT
BAND, THE ARMY BAND, THE FIFE AND DRUM CORPS AND THE
ARMY FIELD BAND) DIFFERS FROM THE ABOVE TABLE.

THEY ARE: SSG(P) AND SFC 30 YEARS; SFC(P) AND 1SG/ MSG 33 YEARS; AND 1SG/MSG(P) AND CSM/SGM 35 YEARS.

(2) COMMAND SERGEANTS MAJOR SERVING IN NOMINA- TIVE POSITIONS WHERE THE COMMANDER IS A LTG OR GEN ARE AUTHORIZED RETENTION BEYOND 30 YEARS. THESE SOLDIERS WILL NOT BE RETAINED BEYOND 35 YEARS TOTAL ACTIVE FED- ERAL SERVICE.

4. CHAPTER 4, AR 635-200, IS CHANGED AS FOLLOWS:

4-4. VOLUNTARY SEPARATION OF SOLDIERS SERVING ON INDEFINITE ENLISTMENTS

A. SOLDIERS DESIRING A VOLUNTARY SEPARATION FOR REASONS NOT SPECIFICALLY COVERED IN THIS REGULATION MUST SUBMIT REQUESTS THROUGH THE SPCMA [Special Court- Martial Authority] TO COMMANDER, PERSCOM [Personnel Com- mand] (TAPC-PDT-PS). IF REQUESTS ARE APPROVED, SOLDIERS WILL BE SEPARATED UNDER THE PROVISIONS OF THIS CHAPTER, AS THEY ARE CONSIDERED TO HAVE FULFILLED THEIR ACTIVE DUTY OBLIGATION.

B. SOLDIERS APPLYING FOR SEPARATION MAY REQUEST SPECIFIC SEPARATION DATES, BUT MUST RECEIVE PRESEPA- RATION COUNSELING NLT [NOT LESS THAN] 90 DAYS BEFORE SEPARATION. REQUESTS FOR SEPARATION DATES MORE THAN 6

MONTHS AFTER THE DATE OF THE APPLICATION MUST BE FULLY
JUSTIFIED.

4-5. CHARACTERIZATION OF SERVICE

A SOLDIER BEING SEPARATED UPON EXPIRATION OF
ENLISTMENT OR FULFILLMENT OF SERVICE OBLIGATION WILL
BE AWARDED A CHARACTER OF SERVICE OF HONORABLE, UNLESS
THE SOLDIER IS IN ENTRY LEVEL STATUS AND SERVICE IS
UNCHARACTERIZED.

4-6. SEPARATION AUTHORITY

SEPARATIONS WILL BE ACCOMPLISHED BY THE TP OR TA
PROCESSING SOLDIER FOR SEPARATION (AR 635-10), PER THE
SEPARATION ORDERS ISSUED BY THE APPROPRIATE COMMANDER.
(SEE AR 600-8-105).

5. THE ARMY LEADERSHIP HAS APPROVED CONVERSION OF
THE QUALITATIVE MANAGEMENT PROGRAM (QMP) FROM A HQDA
BAR TO REENLISTMENT PROGRAM TO A HQDA ADMINISTRATIVE
SEPARATION PROGRAM. ACCORDINGLY, EFFECTIVE UPON PUBLI-
CATION OF NEW EDITION OF AR 635-200, THE PROVISIONS FOR
THE QMP WILL BE MOVED FROM AR 601-280 (CHAPTER 10) TO
AR 635-200. UNTIL AR 635-200 IS PUBLISHED, POLICIES GOV-
ERNING QMP AS LISTED IN CURRENT VERSIONS OF AR 601-280,
DATED 29 SEPTEMBER 1995 WILL CONTINUE TO BE USED. FULL
INSTRUCTIONS CONCERNING QMP AND ITS ADMINISTRATION WILL

BE ISSUED BY THE US ARMY ENLISTED RECORDS AND EVALUA-
TION CENTER (EREC). FOR PLANNING PURPOSES, QMP PROVI-
SIONS UNDER AR 635-200 ARE EXPECTED TO BE IMPLEMENTED IN
THE CALENDAR YEAR 1999 MASTER SERGEANT PROMOTION BOARD,
TENTATIVELY SCHEDULED TO CONVENE 2 FEBRUARY 1999.

6. FULL DETAILS GOVERNING THE INDEFINITE REENLIST-
MENT PROGRAM WILL BE PROVIDED SEPARATELY TO CAREER COUN-
SELORS AND TRANSITION POINTS AS NECESSARY TO MANAGE THE
PROGRAM. SOLDIERS ELIGIBLE TO REENLIST FOR THE INDEFI-
NITE PROGRAM MUST BE IN THE NORMAL REENLISTMENT WINDOW
(12 MONTHS PRIOR TO EXPIRATION TERM OF SERVICE (ETS)
DATE), OR HAVE A SERVICE REMAINING REQUIREMENT. ADDI-
TIONALLY, SOLDIERS WITH OVER 10 YEARS AFS SELECTED FOR
PROMOTION TO SFC, MSG/1SG OR SGM/CSM WILL BE REQUIRED TO
REENLIST FOR INDEFINITE STATUS PRIOR TO BEING PROMOTED.

7. THE INDEFINITE REENLISTMENT PROGRAM IS A POSI-
TIVE STEP BY THE ARMY TO PERMIT CAREER SOLDIERS THE
OPPORTUNITY TO MANAGE THEIR CAREERS MORE EFFECTIVELY
WITHOUT THE UNNECESSARY BURDEN OF RENEWING THEIR CON-
TRACT EVERY FEW YEARS. ONCE ON INDEFINITE STATUS, MOST
SOLDIERS WILL HAVE THE PEACE OF MIND THAT THEY WILL BE
PERMITTED TO SERVE UNTIL MINIMUM RETIREMENT ELIGIBILITY,
OR LONGER CONSISTENT WITH THE RETENTION CONTROL POINT
(RCP) FOR THEIR RANK.

8. THIS MESSAGE CHANGE HAS BEEN APPROVED BY THE SECRETARY OF THE ARMY. POST THIS CHANGE IN FRONT OF THE REGULATION.

9. ODCSPER [Office of the Deputy Chief of Staff, Personnel] POC [POINT OF CONTACT] FOR THE INDEFINITE REENLISTMENT PROGRAM IS SGM PIONK AT DSN: 225-7489, MSG BARBER AT DSN: 225-7490. PERSCOM POC IS MSG PALMATORY AT DSN: 221-6916.

EXPIRES ON: 13AUG99.

BT

********************END RETRANSMISSION********************

2. POC FOR RETRANSMISSION OF THIS MESSAGE IS MSG PALMATORY, DSN 221-6916.

END POLICY MESSAGE 98-19   MSG PALMATORY

Army Message on the Indefinite Reenlistment Program[1]

A Message on the Indefinite Reenlistment Program

From:

Major General Thomas W. Garrett

I am pleased to report to you that the Army's enlisted retention program continues as a "success story" this year.

As the active Army enters the last quarter of fiscal year 1998, it is exceeding its reenlistment goals for initial and mid-term soldiers. This ensures continued high personnel readiness during some turbulent times. We do need your support, however, to meet our goals to retain those soldiers whose active duty obligation ends this fiscal year.

---

[1] This message is online as of January 8, 2007: http://thereupman.tripod.com/id32.htm.

Two key programs have facilitated commanders' reenlistment efforts:

Selective reenlistment bonuses have been a tremendous asset in raising retention rates to historical levels. For example, 11B (Infantryman) is enjoying its best-ever retention rate this year.

Our new automated retention system, RETAIN III, is more responsive than the previous system. It provides more users the ability to access the system simultaneously and provides enhanced reports, a user-friendly interface, multiple task processing and on-line help.

One of the Army's best initiatives to support retention of our career noncommissioned officers—the indefinite reenlistment program—is scheduled for implementation this October.

The program will be mandatory and apply to all Regular Army soldiers in the rank of staff sergeant to command sergeant major who are eligible for reenlistment and have at least 10 or more years of active federal service (AFS) on the date of reenlistment. Soldiers pending a personnel action, such as a MOS medical retention board (MMRB) or reclassification action will be permitted to extend their enlistment for short periods.

In brief, here's how the program will work:

The career counselor will apprise soldiers of their options when they come into the reenlistment window (12 months prior to ETS [expiration of term of service]) or when they must meet a service remaining requirement.

Each soldier will be processed in the RETAIN system, complete all reenlistment documents and take the oath. At that time, the new expiration of term of service date will become the same date as the retention control point for the current rank.

From that point on, whenever the soldier is promoted, the expiration of term of service will be updated to reflect the retention control point for the new rank.

After reenlisting for the indefinite program, a soldier will request voluntary separation or retirement, provided all service remaining requirements have been fulfilled, in a manner similar to officers.

The program is the result of a 1992 Army Deputy Chief of Staff for Personnel (DCSPER) directed study. This study reviewed the merits of an indefinite status for enlisted soldiers. The study found that soldiers (sergeant and below with less than 10 years AFS) who currently had reenlistment options (some skills with a bonus) did not concur with an indefinite status; they preferred to retain their options and bonuses.

On the other hand, career soldiers (staff sergeants and above with 10 or more years [AFS] service who had only the Regular Army option) and senior Army leaders preferred an indefinite status, similar to the current officer program.

In October 1993, the DCSPER approved the recommendation to develop congressional legislation for an enlisted indefinite status. The recommendation was approved in the fiscal year 1997 Defense Authorization Bill.

The guidelines needed to accommodate associated programs, such as assignments, promotions, separations (voluntary, in lieu of permanent change of station and retirements), and ID cards are being finalized. We also have changed other personnel systems, including the RETAIN system, to support the new indefinite status.

We believe implementation of the indefinite reenlistment program is good for the professional NCO Corps, good for the Army, and good for our country. It will bolster the professional NCO Corps image while providing a sense of security for those soldiers committed to the Army; enhance our Army's retention rates; and assure we have a strong "backbone" to support our national military strategy.

Army Policy Message on Processing Indefinite Reenlistment[1]

POLICY MESSAGE 98-21   15 SEPTEMBER 1998

SUBJECT: INDEFINITE REENLISTMENT PROGRAM PROCESS-
ING PROCEDURES.

1. THE INDEFINITE REENLISTMENT PROGRAM WILL BE
IMPLEMENTED ON 1 OCTOBER 1998. REGULAR ARMY SOLDIERS
IN THE RANK OF SSG-CSM WHO WILL HAVE 10 OR MORE YEARS
ACTIVE FEDERAL SERVICE (AFS) ON THE DATE OF DISCHARGE
FOR IMMEDIATE REENLISTMENT WILL BE RESTRICTED TO AN
INDEFINITE TERM OF REENLISTMENT, UNLESS PROHIBITED
BY OTHER PROVISIONS OF AR 601-280. SOLDIERS MENTIONED
ABOVE WILL REENLIST FOR THE INDEFINITE REENLISTMENT
PROGRAM UPON ENTRY INTO THE NORMAL REENLISTMENT WIN-
DOW (12–3 MONTHS PRIOR TO ETS [expiration of term of
service]), OR WHEN REQUIRED TO REENLIST FOR A SERVICE
REMAINING REQUIREMENT. ADDITIONALLY, SOLDIERS OVER

---

[1] This message is online as of January 8, 2007: http://thereupman.tripod.com/id32.htm.

10 YEARS AFS WHO ARE SELECTED FOR PROMOTION TO SFC-CSM WHO WILL HAVE INSUFFICIENT SERVICE REMAINING (24 MONTHS UPON PROMOTION) WILL BE REQUIRED TO REENLIST FOR INDEFINITE STATUS PRIOR TO BEING PROMOTED. SOLDIERS BEING PROMOTED FOR THE MONTH OF OCTOBER 1998 ARE EXEMPT FROM THIS REQUIREMENT.

2. ALTHOUGH THE PROGRAM IS LABELED "INDEFINITE", RETENTION CONTROL POINTS (RCP) FOR THE SOLDIER'S CURRENT OR PROMOTABLE RANK WILL GOVERN THE PERIOD OF ENLISTMENT. RCPs LISTED IN TABLE 3-1, AR 601-280 WILL BE USED TO ESTABLISH THE SOLDIER'S ETS AND WILL AUTOMATICALLY DEFAULT TO THE LAST DAY OF THE MONTH OF THE SOLDIER'S RCP. WHEN COMPUTING THE RCP, DO NOT USE THE 29 DAY RULE. SOLDIERS WHO ARE PROMOTED OR ATTAIN PROMOTION LIST STATUS AFTER THEY HAVE REENLISTED FOR INDEFINITE STATUS WILL AUTOMATICALLY BE ENTITLED TO SERVE UNTIL THE RCP FOR THE NEW RANK AND THE ETS WILL BE UPDATED FROM THE TOP OF THE SYSTEM WITH THE EXCEPTION OF CSM OVER 30 YEARS AND SPECIAL BANDSPERSONS (SEE PARAGRAPH 3 BELOW).

3. WHEN QUALIFYING/DETERMINING ELIGIBILITY FOR INDEFINITE REENLISTMENT, PARTICULAR ATTENTION MUST BE GIVEN TO AGE (NOT TO EXCEED 55), SPECIAL BANDSPERSONS, AND CSM/SGM WITH AUTHORIZED HIGHER RCPs. ALTHOUGH THE LENGTH OF THE CONTRACT IS NORMALLY DETERMINED BY THE RCP, SOLDIERS WHO WILL REACH AGE 55 PRIOR TO THEIR NEW

ETS BASED ON RCP WILL BE RESTRICTED TO WHICHEVER IS
REACHED FIRST. COMMAND SERGEANTS MAJOR SELECTED TO GO
BEYOND 30 YEARS AND SPECIAL BANDSPERSONS WILL BE PRO-
CESSED MANUALLY. THESE REQUESTS WILL BE FORWARDED VIA
HOTLINE CATEGORY "CUSTSERV" FOR RETAIN PROCESSING.

   4. SOLDIERS MAY REPLACE THEIR DD FORM 2 (ACTIVE)
ID CARD UPON REENLISTMENT. SOLDIERS WILL TAKE A COPY
OF THE DD FORM 4 TO THE LOCAL ID CARD ISSUING FACIL-
ITY FOR ISSUANCE OF A NEW ID CARD. EXPIRATION DATE OF
THE NEW ID CARD WILL BE THE RCP DATE AS SHOWN ON THE
DD FORM 4, ITEM 8b (5). SOLDIERS WHO ARE PROMOTED WHILE
SERVING ON INDEFINITE STATUS WILL BE PROCESSED FOR NEW
ID CARD IAW [in accordance with] PROCEDURES ANNOUNCED
IN AR 600-8-14 AND RCPs LISTED IN AR 601-280, PARAGRAPH
3-8G AND TABLE 3-1. ENSURE ALL ID CARD ISSUING FACILI-
TIES RECEIVE A COPY OF THIS MESSAGE.

   5. CASHING IN ACCRUED LEAVE. UPON REENLISTMENT FOR
INDEFINITE STATUS, ACCRUED LEAVE MAY BE CASHED IN, IF
ELIGIBLE. NO PROVISIONS EXIST FOR FURTHER CASHING IN
LEAVE ONCE IN THE PROGRAM UNTIL SOLDIER RETIRES.

   6. CAREER COUNSELORS ARE REMINDED THAT A LEGIBLE
COPY (OR AS REQUIRED) OF THE DD FORM 4 AND OR DA FORM
1695 MUST STILL BE PROVIDED TO THE LOCAL FINANCE OF-
FICE. PERSCOM [Personnel Command] IS CURRENTLY WORK-
ING WITH DFAS [Defense Finance and Accounting Service

(DoD)] ON DEVELOPING PROCEDURES THROUGH AUTOMATION THAT WOULD IN THE FUTURE UPDATE THE SOLDIER'S FINANCE RE-CORDS.

7. RETAIN HAS BEEN MODIFIED TO PROCESS SOLDIERS FOR INDEFINITE STATUS. SOLDIERS WHO MEET THE REQUIRE-MENTS FOR INDEFINITE STATUS WILL BE OFFERED OPTION E-1, REGULAR ARMY REENLISTMENT OPTION. CAREER COUNSEL-ORS WILL BE REQUIRED TO ENTER THE REENLISTMENT DATE AND THE NUMBER OF MONTHS TO TAKE THE SOLDIER TO HIS/ HER RCP YEAR AND MONTH. IF THE NUMBER OF MONTHS EN-TERED IS INCORRECT, THE SYSTEM WILL PROMPT THAT THE RESERVATION HAS FAILED. TO CORRECT THIS, CLICK ON UP-DATE AND THE RETAIN SYSTEM WILL DEFAULT TO THE CORRECT NUMBER OF MONTHS AUTHORIZED, AND AUTOMATICALLY CALCU-LATE THE ETS DATE. TO LOCATE NEW ETS IF DESIRED, GO TO REVIEW SOLDIER, CLICK ON CURRENT SOLDIER STATUS, THEN CLICK ON RESERVATION.

8. THE ENLOP [Enlistment Option] CODE P000 AS SHOWN IN THE EXAMPLE BELOW IS RESERVED FOR INDEFI-NITE STATUS ONLY. RETAIN WILL DEFAULT THE ENLOP CODE TO P000 AT CONFIRMATION. ALSO, IN ITEM 8b (5) OF THE EXAMPLE, WHEN ENTERING THE RCP, ENTER THE LAST DAY OF THE MONTH.

9. PREPARING THE DD FORM 4 SERIES:

   a. ITEM 8, NUMBER OF YEARS ENTER **"INDEFINITE"**

   b. ITEM 8b, EXAMPLE:

   (1) **REGULAR ARMY REENLISTMENT OPTION (P000). RCN:**
1231234

   (2) **NO BONUS ENTITLEMENT**

   (3) **NO WAIVER**

   (4) **4TH REENLISTMENT**

   (5) **"I UNDERSTAND THAT MY REENLISTMENT IS FOR
AN INDEFINITE PERIOD AND THAT I WILL BE ALLOWED TO
SERVE UP TO THE RETENTION CONTROL POINT FOR MY CUR-
RENT RANK. THE RETENTION CONTROL POINT FOR MY CURRENT
RANK IS YY MM DD. I FURTHER UNDERSTAND THAT IF I AM
SELECTED FOR PROMOTION/PROMOTED, REDUCED IN RANK OR
BECOME INELIGIBLE FOR CONTINUED SERVICE THAT I MAY BE
FURTHER RETAINED OR SEPARATED IAW APPROPRIATE POLICIES
IN EFFECT AT THE TIME AS PRESCRIBED BY THE SECRETARY
OF THE ARMY OR APPLICABLE LAW." (INITIALS)**

10. PREPARING DA FORM 3286 PART II:

ITEM 2: ENTER THE OPTION **"REGULAR ARMY"**. ON THE NEXT LINE, ENTER **"IN ACCORDANCE WITH THE NEEDS OF THE ARMY UNDER THE INDEFINITE REENLISTMENT PROGRAM"**.

11. VOLUNTARY SEPARATIONS PRIOR TO RETIREMENT MAY BE REQUESTED FOR SOLDIERS DESIRING TO SEPARATE WHO HAVE COMPLETED ALL SERVICE REMAINING OBLIGATIONS OR ARE REQUESTING SEPARATION IN LIEU OF PCS [permanent change of station]. SEPARATION DATES MUST NOT EXCEED 6 MONTHS FROM DATE OF NOTIFICATION OF ASSIGNMENT INSTRUCTIONS OR MUST BE WITHIN THE COMPLETION OF ANY SERVICE REMAIN-ING OBLIGATIONS OR DEROS [Date Eligible for Return From Overseas] FOR OCONUS [outside the continental United States] BASED SOLDIERS. SOLDIERS MUST RECEIVE PRESEPA-RATION COUNSELING NO LATER THAN 90 DAYS BEFORE SEPA-RATION. APPLICATION FOR SEPARATION DOES NOT GUARANTEE APPROVAL. SEPARATION PROCEDURES IAW CHAPTER 4, AR 635-200 WERE ANNOUNCED IN DAPE-MPE-PD/ALARACT MESSAGE DTG 131810Z AUG 98.

12. REDUCTION IN RANK:

SOLDIERS WITH LESS THAN 20 YEARS ACTIVE FEDERAL SERVICE SERVING INDEFINITE REENLISTMENTS WHO EXCEED RCP AS THE RESULT OF A REDUCTION IN RANK, MAY REMAIN ON ACTIVE DUTY TO ATTAIN RETIREMENT ELIGIBILITY UN-

LESS SEPARATED EARLIER UNDER APPLICABLE ADMINISTRATIVE, PHYSICAL, OR UCMJ [Uniform Code of Military Justice] PROVISIONS.

13. POC [POINT OF CONTACT] AT PERSCOM FOR CA-REER COUNSELOR INQUIRIES IS MSG PALMATORY AT DSN 221-6916. ODCSPER POC IS SGM PIONK OR MSG BARBER AT DSN 225-7489/90. POC FOR ID CARDS IS DAVID KEITH, DSN 221-8941/9590.

END POLICY MESSAGE 98-21   MSG PALMATORY

International Variants of Indefinite Reenlistment

The U.S. Army's indefinite reenlistment program reflects only one way of structuring such a program. The United Kingdom has had an enlistment policy it calls "open engagement" since 1991. As Western European forces have transformed themselves in the past decade from conscript to volunteer forces, several of them have adopted their own variants of an indefinite reenlistment program. An overview of the programs of our Western counterparts reveals alternative ways to structure an indefinite reenlistment program, as well as personnel challenges that may accompany it.

We reviewed the military enlistment policies of nine Western countries with volunteer forces: Australia, Austria, Belgium, Canada, France, Germany, Italy, the Netherlands, and the United Kingdom.[1]

All of these countries have some type of indefinite reenlistment program option for career service members, in addition to a contract option for short-term volunteers. Several also have a contract option for career volunteers that allows service members to renew their service obligation on a periodic basis.

The purpose of the international review was to inform our analysis of indefinite reenlistment policy options by examining program structures, reenlistment incentives including bonuses and pensions, retention issues, and future plans for alternative types of indefinite reenlistment. Enlistment policies of each of the nine countries studied are presented in more detail in the remainder of this appendix.

---

[1] We excluded countries where the primary method of recruitment is conscription (e.g., Denmark, Norway, Sweden, and Switzerland).

An overview of the different combinations of enlistment options we found is provided in Table D.1.

One feature most of these militaries do not have is the attraction of retirement after 20 years of service (around age 40 for most), although they may offer an advantage of an earlier retirement comparable to civilian plans (at age 56 instead of 65, for example, for NCOs in Belgium). The American 20-year retirement program provides great incentive both for those with more than 10 years of service to remain in the military and for those with 20 years of service to leave the service to collect their benefits. This retirement program has come under fire for being inflexible from a force management perspective and for motivating some people who should go to stay until 20 years of service, and some people who should stay beyond 20 years, to leave (Cymrot and Hansen, 2004; DACMC, 2006; Warner, 2006). Thus, the foreign military enlistment programs that do not offer a 20-year retirement are worth considering, not only for their indefinite reenlistment programs but for some of their force management tools as well.

Table D.1
Summary of Enlistment Options in Selected Western Militaries

	Conscription[a]	Short-Term Volunteers	Career: Fixed Contracts	Career: Indefinite Reenlistment
Australia		X	X	X
Austria	X	X		X
Belgium		X		X
Canada		X		X
France		X	X	X
Germany	X	X	X	X
Italy		X	X	X
Netherlands		X	X	X
United Kingdom		X	X	X

[a] In 2005 conscripts accounted for a minority of personnel in these armed forces (Haltiner and Tresch, 2005).

Most of these nations use indefinite reenlistment as a tool for screening, motivating, and/or providing additional benefits to their dedicated career service members. To learn about foreign experiences with indefinite reenlistment programs, we reviewed official Web sites and the broader literature, and we conducted interviews with personnel from the respective militaries who are knowledgeable about military careers, related issues such as evaluation and manning, and future military career concepts and policies in general. The interviews and reviews were conducted in Dutch, English, French, and German.

We made initial contact with the majority of our interview participants through their embassies in London, where we approached the military attachés with a request for information.[2] In these cases, the military attachés were able to either provide us with the required information or refer us to appropriate in-country military contacts. Other successful approaches of initiating contact included general inquiries through the appropriate military Web sites and visits to local army recruitment centers. Most notable is the fact that indefinite reenlistment options, whether long employed or newly instituted, are common in Western militaries with all-volunteer forces. Unlike the American Army program, several of these programs require testing, education, or competitive selection in order for military personnel to be given indefinite status. Furthermore, indefinite reenlistment is typically coupled with additional privileges and benefits, which would likely boost personnel prestige as well.[3]

---

[2] A contact list of Commonwealth defence liaison staffs and foreign service attachés accredited to London can be found in *The White Book of the U.K. Ministry of Defence* at http://www.mod.uk/publications/whitebook/azindex.htm.

[3] An independent assessment of the impact of these programs on the quality and prestige of senior enlisted personnel was beyond the scope of this study.

Australia

Enlistment Structure

The Australian Defence Forces are composed of an all-volunteer force and typically employ a mix of fixed-term and "open engagement" contracts for service personnel. Both enlisted and officer ranks complete an initial period of service based on the amount of training received; for enlisted personnel, the initial period of service is four years when initial training is shorter than 26 weeks, 6 years when initial training is longer than 26 weeks.[4] Once this initial period of bound service is complete, the service offers the majority of its members an open engagement contract (i.e., indefinite reenlistment), and they are free to stay as long as they wish or to leave after a six-month notice period. However, service members with questionable performance during their initial engagement may be offered only a fixed-period contract instead of being granted career service status. This program was recently challenged for not offering enough incentives to compel personnel to stay beyond their initial term of enlistment.

Reenlistment Incentives, Retention, and Force Planning

Bonuses are offered to certain members of occupational specialties with low retention rates, such as pilots, air traffic controllers, submariners, and aerospace engineers. But these bonuses "are viewed as a short term holding mechanism while other long-term measures are put in place [to enhance retention]."[5]

The Australian military retirement system mandates retirement at 55 years of age, compared with age 60 in the civilian community. Pensions also commence at 55, regardless of years of service. The retirement entitlement amount is based on the number of years of service and the service member's average salary over the last three years of service.

---

[4] Typically, nontechnical trades have shorter training periods than the technical trades, and thus have shorter initial periods of service.

[5] Brian Adams, head of Defence Personnel Executive for the Australian Department of Defence, interview with Joy Moini, March 24, 2004.

Since the 1990s, the Australian Defence Forces have experienced serious problems meeting recruiting and retention goals. The problems with retention are seen as being caused by service members' quality-of-life concerns, including work and family conflicts, longer working hours because of personnel shortages, and the civilianization and out-sourcing of military jobs, which has made military pay less competitive and remaining military jobs less desirable. The single career track offered by the open engagement contract system is seen as too inflexible to meet the demands of some service members, and there is no incentive to stay beyond the initial obligation for most occupational specialties. This causes high numbers of personnel to leave just as they develop experience and knowledge of the job and makes it difficult for services to assess manning levels and future needs—a concern with the indefinite reenlistment system raised by the U.S. Air Force representatives we interviewed.

In response to concerns about the low rates of retention, in 1998 the Australian Department of Defence (DOD) initiated a new Flexible Career Management System (FCMS), which comprised initiatives designed to add greater flexibility and more options for service members and career managers. A major component of the FCMS was the introduction of fixed periods of service that would replace open-ended enlistment contracts for all personnel entering the service after July 1, 1998. The "phased careers" would be supported by financial incentives upon completion of each period of service. Upon further analysis, however, the DOD concluded that this was not a cost-effective solution to the retention problem. The administrative burden of managing the new system as well as the financial obligation necessary to provide the new incentives made the fixed-contract concept untenable compared with the existing system. The DOD has since moved away from fixed periods of service in favor of open-ended engagements. However, it has continued to support other flexible employment programs as a way to entice personnel to stay in the services. These programs include

- permanent part-time employment at prorated pay for difficult-to-fill staff positions

- job sharing, where two or more people each work part time to complete the requirements of one job
- variable working hours, used to facilitate service members' education or training or to meet family needs such as dependent care
- temporary home-located work under certain circumstances, such as convalescence
- transfer of personnel between services
- a defense-industry personnel exchange program.

These initiatives work alongside open-ended contracts to improve retention in the career force.

Austria

Enlistment Structure
In Austria a minimum of eight months of military service is compulsory for males aged 18 and over. After conscription, personnel can choose to extend their period of service as temporary career volunteers on fixed-term contracts. The fixed term is typically three years and is twice renewable for a maximum of nine years. Following the term of conscription and nine years of serving as a volunteer, personnel can apply for enlistment as regular career soldiers, subject to suitability and demand. The attainment of "full regular status" (career status) requires a commitment of six more years of service and a posting abroad.

Reenlistment Incentives, Retention, and Force Planning
Personnel do not receive enlistment bonuses of any kind; instead, the incentive to reenlist is considered the status achieved as a regular soldier, which grants civil servant status and offers guaranteed employment until retirement. Personnel receive full state benefits only when they reach the career status of regular soldier. Benefits for regular soldiers include health care and a state pension. Austrian pension reform in 2004 set the regular pension age at 60 to 65 and ruled that, beginning in 2017, there will be a universal pension age of 65. Given the attractive benefits attained only by reaching career service status (job

security, pension, and health care), it is very rare for those who have achieved the status of regular soldier to leave the armed forces before retirement.

The almost full retention rates of regular soliders facilitate the planning of future personnel needs. However, there is concern that the late pension age of regular soldiers leads to an age structure that is incompatible with the requirements of a modern army. To counteract the resulting aging of the armed forces, more shorter-term contracts for younger personnel have been introduced.

Belgium

Enlistment Structure

Three engagement options are available to Belgium's armed forces, including a short-term option, a long-term but limited career option, and long-term full-career option. The short-term option includes one year of training followed by one year of service, after which personnel can reenlist in one-year increments for five to seven years of service until age 25.

There are two types of long-term engagement options: the limited career and the full career. The long-term limited-career option allows enlisted soldiers to become NCOs and NCOs to become officers by passing an exam, but there is a limit on the highest rank obtainable. Personnel who wish to pursue the higher ranks and an even longer career must then pass another exam to achieve full status. This long-term full-career option is competitive; it is available only to a limited number of personnel. Once on the long-term full-career engagement, personnel are still subject to a four-year probationary period.

Some exceptional new recruits are accepted directly into the long-term full-career option. They typically enter the service at age 18, and during the probationary period they are evaluated on their physical condition, professional knowledge, and moral quality. Indefinite enlistment until retirement at the age of 56 years is ensured on passing the evaluation at the end of the fourth year of service.

There is no direct option for those on short-term engagements to switch to the long-term service. However, if they fulfill the engagement requirements for the full-career option (i.e., serve a four-year probationary period, pass the evaluation, and complete an education requirement), they can take advantage of a number of reserved long-term engagements.

Reenlistment Incentives, Retention, and Force Planning
In general, there are no provisions for enlistment and reenlistment bonuses, although extra allowances are provided in addition to salary for certain occupations with skill shortages. For those on long-term service engagements, the financial incentive is considered the higher retirement payments that result from longer periods of service.

The pension structure is an attractive feature of a military career. The retirement age, which depends on the occupation and the rank obtained, starts at 56 years for NCOs and compares well with the retirement age of 65 years for civilian jobs in the private and public sectors. The amount of military retirement pay is also attractive; this can be a maximum of 75 percent of the final year's salary. (Civilian public-sector retirement pay is calculated based on the last five years of salary.) The maximum pension can be obtained after 37.5 years of military service, which compares favorably to 45 years of service for civilian public-sector occupations.

The Belgian military is currently facing difficulty in recruiting younger personnel for short-term engagements and in recruiting NCOs for certain technical functions. Generally, like the Austrian military, the Belgian military is facing the challenge of an aging force structure.

The short-term option, which was introduced in 1994 following the end of conscription to continue to provide the Army with young combat personnel, has not enlisted the desired number of personnel to meet annual recruitment needs. The difficulties faced by personnel in returning to civilian life are viewed as a drawback of the short-term option and may affect recruitment numbers. Currently the military does not have the resources to provide services to aid personnel in the transition.

The aging force structure was largely brought about because a 16 percent downsizing of the military (following the suspension of conscription in 1994) was administered through a reduction in the annual enlistment quota without compulsory early retirement. In response to the trends in its age distribution, the Belgian military will introduce a "mixed-career" option to replace the current structure by 2008. It will likely include a four-year minimum period of service or probationary period and an option to serve until age 40. Between the ages of 35 and 40, all personnel will have their performance evaluated. Based on the evaluation and the individual's preferences, three options are possible:

- Personnel will be retained until military retirement at age 56.
- Personnel will transfer to a civilian job in the military or another state department until civilian retirement at age 65.
- Personnel will be requested to separate from the military at age 40.

This mixed-career option is designed to allow more flexibility for force planners to achieve demographic structural changes. The aim is to bring the average age of military members to below 30 years, from the current average of 37.5.

Canada

Enlistment Structure

The Canadian Forces (CF) began a major reform of the engagement structure for enlisted personnel in 1998 to address problems it anticipated in recruiting and retention due to shifting demographics and changes in the operational environment. Inadequate distribution of rank, experience, and skills in certain occupations revealed the difficulties in retention, and the CF believed the existing term of service (TOS) structure was contributing to the problem.[6] Some of the major

---

[6]   Director, Military Employment Policy, "From Project Inception to Option Analysis, June 1998–May 2001," Canadian Forces Regular Force Terms of Service Review Project, May 2001.

challenges cited were retention concerns, personnel expectations, and the need for flexibility and adaptability.[7] The new engagement structure was implemented on May 1, 2005. It consists of four components: The Variable Initial Engagement, the Intermediate Engagement 25, the Indefinite Period of Service, and the Continuing Engagement.

The Variable Initial Engagement (VIE) is a three- to nine-year term, depending on occupation, and serves as an entry point for enlisted personnel. The VIE replaces the Basic Initial Engagement, which was exclusively a three-year contract. The CF seek to strike a balance between recovering the training costs invested in personnel by ensuring service of an appropriate length while offering an attractive option to potential recruits who might be discouraged by a long commitment requirement.[8]

The second stage is the Intermediate Engagement 25 (IE25), for which personnel are selected based on performance criteria (in most cases) to serve for an indefinite period of up to 25 years of service. Previously the Intermediate Engagement called for 20 years of service, but the TOS review found that 20 years of service did not maximize the cost-effectiveness of training and experience investments in personnel. The CF are experiencing a tenure problem because of personnel cutbacks in the mid-1990s and expect that extending the required service from 20 to 25 years will help to address the experience gap it faces.

The Indefinite Period of Service (IPS) engagement is available to personnel after the VIE or the IE25, based on performance, and typically implies service until the compulsory retirement age, which was recently raised from 55 to 60. The intent of the original IPS, introduced in the 1970s, was to release 80 percent of personnel at or before 20 years of service and provide the remaining 20 percent with job security until retirement. However, it was never fully implemented and was rarely used until recently, when the CF revisited the TOS structure in its comprehensive 1998 review. The CF now envision granting IPS status to professionals such as lawyers and social workers, because

[7] Canadian Forces Regular Force Terms of Service Review Project, "The New Structure: A Primer," August 2004.

[8] ADM (HR-Mil) Instruction, Annex B, August 2004.

many such specialists begin their careers with the military relatively later in life, and the job security offered by the IPS is a retention incentive for them. The CF will also grant IPS status after 25 years of service to some personnel on the IE25 engagement as a way to retain the best performers.

Both IPS and IE25 members can voluntarily separate from the service, and the service can release personnel if necessary. Service members must give 30 days' advance notice if they are entitled to an immediate retirement annuity, six months if they have not yet achieved that entitlement, which depends on years of service. In the latter case, the member may be entitled to a deferred retirement annuity, or a prorated annuity amount. Under provisions of the National Defence Act, the CF can hold a member in service for up to one year, or it can release service members for medical reasons or disciplinary actions with any amount of notice it chooses. The CF can also release personnel for reasons of economy and efficiency when an occupation is overmanned; in these cases, service members are entitled to an immediate annuity if they are vested, and they are given notice of one year.

Finally, the CF have a flexible term of service called the Continuing Engagement (CE), which is available after the VIE and IE25 for any length of time the service requires. Previously the CE term was set at five years, but under the new system it will provide the services with flexibility to meet the needs of under- and overmanned occupations on a temporary or long-term basis.[9]

Reenlistment Incentives, Retention, and Force Planning

The CF are facing a difficult demographic problem in the near future, when there will be a large number of service personnel retirements. A previous dip in the number of recruits, coupled with the approaching retirement of the current generation, is expected to cause a personnel shortage. The Canadians also anticipate challenges filling leadership roles, as personnel are not hired in laterally. In response, the CF

---

[9] "TOS Instruction Comments," August 2004; Canadian Forces Regular Force Terms of Service Review Project, "The New Structure: A Primer," August 2004.

increased the years of service required for full retirement by five years and are reconsidering the option of offering retention bonuses.[10]

Historically, retention bonuses have not been necessary in the CF as attrition rates tend to be quite low. Previously, retention bonuses were provided only to pilots in the Air Force, but even those were discontinued because the bonus was not judged to be cost-effective. In general, the CF do not believe bonuses are a cost-effective retention tool because they require payment to 100 percent of the group regardless of how many of them intended to leave. Instead, the Canadians would like to create a "culture of retention," which involves antecedents of retention they have identified, such as career planning, move policies, and promotions. The CF believe their retention problems are related to perceptions of unfair practices in these areas, and would rather take measures to address misperceptions than offer bonuses across the board to increase retention.

The Canadian Forces Superannuation Act of 2001 changed the law governing pension policy to provide benefits to service members who have 25 years of cumulative service rather than the 20 years or more of continuous service that had been established previously. This legislative change provides the CF with more flexibility in managing the force and provides a retention incentive for service members to stay past the 20-year point.[11] To achieve the maximum available pension of 70 percent of salary one must complete 35 years of service.

France

Enlistment Structure
In the French Army, service options are enlisted soldier, temporary or regular NCO, and temporary or regular officer. The army is composed

---

[10] Douglas A. Lock, Manager, Military HR Policy development, and Director, Military Employment Policy (DMEP 4), interview with Joy Moini, August 2004.

[11] Unlike in the American system, all Canadian soldiers contribute to a retirement system, and those who leave prior to 20 years of service are entitled to a return of all of their retirement contributions.

entirely of volunteers, as conscription was phased out between 1996 and 2001.

Enlisted soldiers have the option of an initial engagement of 3 to 5 years, for a maximum period of service of 22 years. Temporary NCOs are recruited from among the enlisted soldiers as well as from the civilian sector to serve for an initial period of 5 to 10 years, depending on the amount and type of training provided, up to the retirement age of 57. Regular NCOs are recruited from among the pool of temporary NCOs who have served between 5 and 8 years and who have successfully passed an exam. They then obtain a status comparable to that of civil servants and serve until retirement at age 57.

A small number of temporary officers are also selected from among the NCOs and civilians to fill vacant junior officer positions. These temporary officers are enlisted for an initial period of 2 to 5 years and can renew their contracts for up to 15 years. In the case of enlistment as a specialist temporary officer (e.g., a linguist or a technician), the initial period of service is also 2 to 5 years, but the maximum length of contract service is 20 years. Both of these groups of temporary officers are eligible for regular officer status during or after the completion of the contracted period of service.

Reenlistment Incentives, Retention, and Force Planning
Common soldiers and temporary NCOs who serve for a period of five years are offered a number of retention incentives. Personnel can choose their next service location and receive quality-of-life benefits such as improved accommodations and promotions. Service members who have served a minimum of five years also receive guaranteed support for their transition into civilian life should they choose to leave the army. This support includes paid internships during service, assistance with job searches, and employer incentives for hiring veterans.

Soldiers are entitled to a pension if they have served for a minimum period of 15 years. The pension levels are better than in the civilian sector, though not strictly comparable, as the Army offers shorter careers and a wider scope for promotion on the basis of years of service.

According to French officials we interviewed, the present arrangements for recruitment, retention, and pensions are working well. There is high demand for the status of regular NCO, and officers with regular status rarely leave the army before retirement. The appeal of the security and long-term perspective of regular status is thought to outweigh possible negative effects on motivation, especially because regular NCOs and officers still look forward to promotion. It can, however, be a challenge to retain senior NCOs with specialist training that is attractive to employers in the civilian sector, such as those with mechanical skills. Retention incentives for this group currently include faster promotions and higher salaries. Futhermore, the French Army is currently considering increasing pay and financial rewards for personnel with qualifications that are in demand in the civilian sector.

Germany

Enlistment Structure
The German Armed Forces require national service of nine months for males aged 18 and over. After conscription, personnel can choose to extend their period of service by 1 to 14 months as short-term volunteers or enlist as temporary career volunteers on fixed-term contracts for periods of 2, 4, 6, 8, 12, or 15 years to a maximum of 20 years. After serving for a typical period of 6 years as a temporary career soldier, and depending on performance and demand, personnel can apply for permanent enlistment as regular soldiers. Candidates for officers' training who perform exceptionally well on the entry exam can also obtain a guarantee to be awarded the status of regular soldier on completion of training without previously serving as temporary career soldiers.

Reenlistment Incentives, Retention, and Force Planning
To make military service more appealing to existing and new staff, an Attractiveness Program of salary increases and faster promotions was introduced in 2002 as one of a number of structural changes. Other reforms in 2002 included an extended internal training program and "side-door" entry points (i.e., lateral entry) for specialist staff from the

civilian sector. Personnel, however, do not receive enlistment bonuses of any kind; instead, the incentive to reenlist is considered the status achieved as a regular soldier, which offers guaranteed employment until retirement and attractive health benefits and pensions. Pensions mirror those available to civil servants and are considered attractive. Retirement occurs at the age of 41, 55, or 60, depending on rank and occupation.

It is very rare for regular soldiers to leave the German Armed Forces before retirement. The different contracts available to temporary and career soldiers and an internal job fair allow flexible planning, and the current recruitment situation is considered favorable. However, there is some recognition of the possibility that the long-term employment guarantee given to career soldiers may not encourage good performance to the same extent as shorter-term contracts or bonuses. Moreover, some aspirant officers who sign 12-year contracts return to the civilian sector prematurely after having benefited from Armed Forces–funded university education, paying a relatively small penalty for not completing the agreed period of service. Similarly, there is a risk that highly skilled regular soldiers, such as pilots, will terminate their contracts at a later stage to take advantage of more lucrative salaries offered by commercial employers.

Italy

Enlistment Structure

Legislative changes in 1995 aimed at increasing recruitment and retention of Italian Army enlisted personnel transformed the grade and promotion structure of the Italian military as it works toward phasing out conscription by 2006. The legislation first increased TOS for junior enlisted personnel called *volontari in ferma breve* (VFB, or short-term volunteers) from two to three years, with the option to recommit every two years, and later introduced five-year terms in 2002. At the end of the VFB term, personnel who have performed well are offered a position in the career force and become *volontari in servizio perman-*

ente (VSP, or career service volunteers). Those reaching VSP status can remain in the service for life because there are no up-or-out rules.

The army also includes enlisted volunteers who sign on for a period of 12 months; those volunteers, called *volontari in ferma annuale* (VFA, or annual contract volunteers), are paid less than short-term volunteers but more than conscripts and have priority for short-term volunteer billets after their initial term is over. A fourth type of enlisted volunteer is the marshal, similar to our warrant officer, who is a part of the career force (Zanini, 2002). Personnel promoted from the short-term volunteer ranks fill 30 percent of the marshal positions, while the remaining 70 percent are reserved for lateral entrants from the civilian sector.

Reenlistment Incentives, Retention, and Force Planning

Although Italy experienced a surge of applicants for voluntary military service at the end of the draft in 1999, there has been a decline recently because of competition for recruits with the civilian National Service. The National Service offers government or nonprofit employment for one year for Italian citizens between the ages of 18 and 28. In response, the Ministry of Defense increased the pay and benefits for recruits and offers guaranteed employment in the public or private sector after service (Stroud and Omeltchenko, 2003).

Army personnel are eligible for retirement benefits when they reach either age 60 or 37 years of service.[12] Personnel who choose to leave the service before that point receive retirement contributions earned over the length of their service as part of their social security benefits.

The Italian Army has experienced fairly low retention rates with low-level VFB personnel, as many opt to join the police forces after their first term in the military.[13] Overall, however, retention in the Italian Army is high, though the data available to us are somewhat limited.

---

[12] The eligibility requirement for retirement benefits will increase to 40 years of service in 2007.

[13] Recruitment is managed jointly by the military services and the police forces, which together recruit individuals to perform military service in exchange for a guarantee of employment with the police after retirement.

The Netherlands

Enlistment Structure

Following the end of conscription in 1996, the Dutch armed forces were transformed into an all-volunteer force while simultaneously downsizing and restructuring. The new personnel policy is aimed at ensuring flexibility, professionalism, and a reduction in the age of personnel. This requires an increase in the proportion of fixed-term service contracts. The goal of the Dutch armed forces is to retain 60 percent of all service personnel on short-term contracts.

There are now two engagement models for military personnel: short-term and unlimited contracts. Initial short-term contracts vary in length depending on service. For the army, initial contract length varies from 2.5 to 11 years. The initial contract can be followed by another limited contract with a maximum of 18 years that is offered only to personnel between the ages of 17 and 35. Selected personnel who exhibit good performance may be allowed to transfer to an unlimited contract. Unlimited contracts are available to select personnel after a six-month probation period. The minimum duration of unlimited contracts is the training period plus two times the training period (with a minimum of 5 years and a maximum of 7). After this period, personnel on unlimited contracts are permitted to leave the service with three months' notice.

Reenlistment Incentives, Retention, and Force Planning

No bonuses are paid to personnel in the unlimited contract engagement because of the need to reduce the percentage of such contracts and achieve an overall reduction of personnel. However, personnel on short-term contracts are offered bonuses for hard-to-fill jobs in certain occupations. Under both short-term and unlimited contracts, personnel can leave the military and return later. If they are absent for fewer than six years, their salary upon return will be the same as if they had served those years.

Personnel on unlimited contracts generally serve until retirement at age 55 (age 50 for the navy). The retirement age is to be gradually raised to 58 by 2011. For the period between retirement and age 65, retirement payment is 80 percent of the final year's salary. Beyond the age of 65 years, the pension amount takes into account the number of years of service. The conditions for early retirement are much better for military personnel than for civilians (although the minimum age for entering the retirement system is being raised). Overall, Dutch military retirement policy is considered a positive element of a military career in the Netherlands.

Personnel on unlimited contracts generally serve until retirement at age 55, so there are few difficulties with retention. The current challenge facing the Dutch military is to increase the percentage of short-term contracts to 60 percent and to reduce the long-term contracts to 40 percent, resulting in a larger proportion of younger people in the lower ranks. Recent trends suggest that the proportions are changing in the desired direction (see Figure D.1). In support of this goal, the services actively approach short-term personnel at the end of their contract and usually offer a renewal, depending on the needs of the service and the ability of the individual.

The United Kingdom

Enlistment Structure

On January 1, 1991, the United Kingdom introduced a new enlistment program, called Open Engagement, for all new recruits. It replaced the old program, Notice Engagement, which was in place from 1952 to 1990. Under Notice Engagement, soldiers were given the option of signing on for 3, 6, 9, 12, or 22 years, with conditions of service and pay varying with the length of their commitment. A 12-month notice for separation was required under the program. The administrative burden associated with Notice Engagement was large, as the army had to actively retain soldiers beyond the notice period. The line management function was used to switch soldiers to longer periods of engagement to increase retention rates and reduce administration. Soldiers still on Notice Engagement are eligible to apply for premature voluntary release or repayment. Currently approximately 30 percent of soldiers remain on Notice Engagement.

Figure D.1
Trend in the Shares of Short-Term and Long-Term Contracts as Percentages of the Total for the Dutch Military

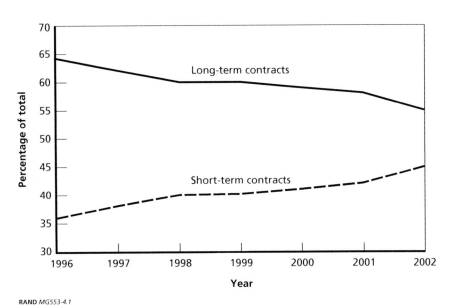

RAND *MG553-4.1*

Under Open Engagement, all recruits sign on for a full 22-year career. They must normally serve for a minimum of four years, and 12 months' notice is required to leave. Once soldiers have completed the full term of their career, the opportunity to extend their service beyond 22 years is open to selected individuals. Regular formal career reviews are held to judge each soldier's continued suitability for a full career of 22 years. If a soldier is no longer deemed suitable, he or she can be discharged after 12 months' notice at the 6-, 9-, and 12-year manning control points (MCPs).

Reenlistment Incentives: Bonuses and Pensions

Every soldier serving on an Open Engagement receives commitment bonus financial retention incentives (FRIs). Two payments are made as part of this initiative: 3,000 GBP ($5,500) at the five-year point and 2,500 GBP ($4,600) at the eight-year point. The payment is automatic and is designed to reward length of service. Such a scheme is expensive, because payment is made to everyone, even soldiers who had no intention of leaving.

FRIs are also used as a tactical measure to retain trained personnel and address manpower shortages in specific career employment groups. For example, FRIs exist to address manpower shortages in the Royal Signals trades and in aircrew.[14] Military skill shortages appear in areas that are in demand in the civilian workforce, such as information technology, medicine, and aviation. Training return of service clauses also exist whereby personnel trained by the army must serve a minimum number of years, depending on the course of training undertaken; the longest term is five years.

The UK military pension is considered among the best in the country. The pension has some limited value as a recruiting tool, but much greater effect as an incentive for those with significant service to continue to the 22-year point. After serving for the full 22 years under Open Engagement, a soldier receives an immediate pension, which consists of a tax-free lump sum equal to approximately 90 percent of the final annual gross basic pay, plus a monthly taxed income for life of approximately 30 percent of the final gross basic pay. A soldier leaving the army with insufficient service for an immediate pension is entitled to a preserved pension provided that at least two years have been served. The preserved pension commences at age 60 and consists of a lump sum plus monthly payments, the rates of which are dependent on time served. This pension scheme is currently being reviewed.

Retention and Force Planning

Increasing the minimum term of engagement from three to four years with the move from Notice Engagement to Open Engagement has led to better retention levels of UK regular forces. Indeed, there has been a decrease in the outflow from the regular forces since 1993.

---

[14] To address manpower shortages in Royal Signals trades, payments are made on successful completion of specific courses. The Aircrew retention review FRI package comprises a series of payments (introduced in 2002) and a new, separate Professional Aviator's pay structure created in April 2003 for selected aircrew in the army who are part of the Pilot Employment Stream (source: http://www.army.mod.uk).

There are also drawbacks to the Open Engagement option. Beyond the 12-year MCP, soldiers are entitled to complete 22 years of service, which presents inflexibilities in managing the personnel structure between the 12- and 22-year points. The current length of service, between four years and 12 years, is below the steady (target) state, and service between 13 years and 22 years is above the target state. In its attempts to use the MCP system to move the current personnel structure toward the desired structure, however, the army has come under criticism for discharging soldiers who have completed more than 12 years of service earlier than they had aspired to leave (i.e., before serving 22 years).

In an effort to further improve retention levels and manage the age structure, a Versatile Engagement (VENG) option is being considered, based on an up-or-out strategy. The VENG will be a modification to the current Open Engagement option, which will consist of a nine-year engagement with a minimum of four years of service and a one-year notice period. Depending on the performance of the individual and the manning requirements of the army, the contract may be extended to 12, 15, 22, or a maximum of 35 years. Committal bonuses are expected to be a core part of this option.

The central aims of the proposed VENG option are to

- provide a flexible, integrated career structure that allows soldiers to serve beyond 22 years (for up to 35 years of service) in certain circumstances and categories
- improve the retention of soldiers beyond four years of service
- ensure better use of experienced soldiers through wider employment and more flexible terms of service.

Extending the term of service to 35 years under VENG is believed to be particularly appropriate where high training costs are incurred or where physical demands are not paramount, because a cost saving is identified with employing people for longer periods of time, as fewer personnel would need to be recruited and trained. The full details of the VENG option are still under consideration, and the option is likely to come into effect on January 1, 2008.[15]

Conclusion

A summary of the details of the nine Western military enlistment programs is given in Table D.2. The second column of the table describes the standard enlistment contracts for each country, and the rest of the columns describe the indefinite reenlistment programs. Notably, indefinite reenlistment options, whether long employed or newly instituted, are common in Western militaries with all-volunteer forces. Particularly appealing may be the programs that offer a combination of fixed-contract and career-status enlistment programs, where the career status is accompanied by better pay and benefits and must be achieved through passing some sort of test or meeting certain performance criteria. The fixed-contract force can serve as the pool that is contracted or expanded to meet the size requirements of the force or certain professions without having to involuntarily separate career soldiers or bear the expense of separation pay. The challenge would be to determine the optimal size of the career pool to maintain the proper age distribution within the force while honoring commitments to allow career soldiers to serve until retirement.

---

[15] This date coincides with the introduction of an automated administrative system.

Table D.2
Comparison of Western Military Enlistment Programs

Country–Service	Standard Enlistment Contracts	Indefinite Reenlistment (IR) Program	Eligibility for IR Status	Mandatory or Optional	Minimum Obligation	Bonus	Advance Notice for Separation	Number of Participants
United States–Army	4 to 6 years	Army indefinite reenlistment	10 years of service and grade E-6–E-9	Mandatory	Not linked to IR status	No	6 months	88,637 (22% of enlisted force)
Australia[a]	4 years	Open engagement contracts	Completion of bound service period	Mandatory	None	No	6 months	Not available
Austria–Armed Forces[b]	3 years	Regular soldier status	All non-commissioned officers who successfully complete training receive civil servant status and are expected to serve until retirement	Mandatory	1 month	No	For soldiers giving notice, 1 month. If the military initiates the separation, notice within the first 6 years of service varies between 1 and 3 months, depending on length of service. If soldiers have attained full regular status (after serving for 6 years and serving abroad), they cannot be dismissed.	16,000 (46% of force)

Table D.2—Continued

Country–Service	Standard Enlistment Contracts	Indefinite Reenlistment (IR) Program	Eligibility for IR Status	Mandatory or Optional	Minimum Obligation	Bonus	Advance Notice for Separation	Number of Participants
Belgium–Armed Forces[c]	1 to 2 years; 13 to 16 years for some specialty occupations	Long-term full-career status (militaires de carrière)	After a 4-year probationary period, passing an evaluation of professional knowledge, physical condition, moral quality, and medical fitness	Optional. Can sign on for service until retirement at 56 years of age.	Minimum of 3 years, maximum of 12 years (1.5 times the duration of the education and training paid for by the military)	Yes, for certain occupations	Personnel must normally give 3 months' notice to leave the military, but if there is no administrative delay and the Minister of Defense agrees, personnel can leave after 1 month. The military can initiate separation only in certain rare circumstances.	37,335 (91% of total military strength of the armed forces)
Canada–Armed Forces[d]	3 to 9 years	Indefinite period of service (IPS)	Selection from those who have completed initial engagement, intermediate engagement, or continuing engagement contracts	Optional	No	No	30 days if eligible for immediate retirement annuity, 6 months if not	Not available (program new in 2005)

Table D.2—Continued

Country–Service	Standard Enlistment Contracts	Indefinite Reenlistment (IR) Program	Eligibility for IR Status	Mandatory or Optional	Minimum Obligation	Bonus	Advance Notice for Separation	Number of Participants
France / Army[e]	1 to 5 years, depending on type of soldier	Regular non-commissioned officers status (NCOs)	For temporary NCOs, 5 to 8 years of service and passing an exam	Optional	Typically 5 to 8 years	No, but temporary NCOs are able to stipulate certain conditions, such as place of relocation, when renewing their contracts	2 to 3 months for NCOs giving notice	48,000 (36% of force)

Table D.2—Continued

Country–Service	Standard Enlistment Contracts	Indefinite Reenlistment (IR) Program	Eligibility for IR Status	Mandatory or Optional	Minimum Obligation	Bonus	Advance Notice for Separation	Number of Participants
Germany–Armed Forces[f]	4 to 20 years	Regular soldier status	Typically 6 years of service or scoring well on an officers' entry exam and successfully passing a subsequent training module	Optional	Short-service volunteers can serve from 1 to 14 months; temporary-career soldiers enlist for 2 years or more	No	The military cannot dismiss regular soldiers before the end of their contracts, except in cases of misconduct. Soldiers giving notice can request the date of separation; the maximum notice period is 3 months (for a soldier giving notice on the grounds that a continued career will cause personal, professional, or economic hardship).	59,750 (21.6% of force)
Italy–Armed Forces[g]	2 to 5 years	Career force status	Completion of initial period of service	Optional	None	No	No	28,204

Table D.2—Continued

Country–Service	Standard Enlistment Contracts	Indefinite Reenlistment (IR) Program	Eligibility for IR Status	Mandatory or Optional	Minimum Obligation	Bonus	Advance Notice for Separation	Number of Participants
Netherlands[h]	Initial short-term contracts vary between 2.5 years (lower ranks) and 11 years (higher ranks)	Long-term engagement	Completion of 6-month probation period	Optional	Training period plus 2 times the training period, with a minimum of 5 years and a maximum of 7 years	No (recently discontinued)	3 months' notice	28,872 (55% of force) in 2002
United Kingdom–Army[i]	Open engagement (1991 to present); former version, in place from 1952 to 1990, required a minimum of 3 years of service	22 years; reviewed at the 6-, 9-, and 12-year points	Minimum of 4 years of service before signing on for 22 years of service	Optional	4 years of service	Yes, at the 5- and 8-year points	12 months' notice after at least 3 years have been served	58,000 (68% of non-commissioned force)

Table D.2—Continued

[a] Department of National Defence and Canadian Forces, 2001. This report reviews terms of other nations' programs, including that of Australia.

[b] Representative from the Austrian Ministry of Defense

[c] Representative from Human Resources at the Belgium Ministry of Defense.

[d] Representative from the Department of National Defence and Canadian Forces, "New Terms of Service Now in Effect," *Canadian Forces Personnel Newsletter*, Issue 5/05, May 2005, available at http://www.forces.gc.ca/hr/cfpn/engraph/5_05/5_05_tos_e.asp.

[e] Military representative from the French Embassy in London.

[f] Representative from the German Federal Ministry of Defense.

[g] Zanini, 2002.

[h] Representative from the Dutch Ministry of Defense; Integrale Monitor Personeelsvoorziening Defensie, 2002; Dutch Ministry of Defense, 2003.

[i] Representative from Manning (Army) at the United Kingdom Ministry of Defensce.

Bibliography

Agg, J., "Selection Board Helps to Process First-Term Re-Enlistment Packages," n.d., http://www.quantico.usmc.mil/PAO1/Sentry%20Copy%202003/21%20Aug/Selection%20board%20helps%20to%20process%20first.htm (as of March 30, 2006).

Army Regulation 635-200, Chapter 4, paragraph 4-4.

Asch, Beth, Can Du, and Matthias Schonlau, *Policy Options for Military Recruiting in the College Market*, Santa Monica, Calif.: RAND Corporation, 2004.

Asch, Beth, and James R. Hosek, *Looking to the Future: What Does Transformation Mean for Military Manpower and Personnel Policy?* Santa Monica, Calif.: RAND Corporation, 2004.

Asch, Beth, James R. Hosek, Jeremy Arkes, C. Christine Fair, Jennifer Sharp, and Mark Totten, *Military Recruiting and Retention After the Fiscal Year 2000 Military Pay Legislation*, Santa Monica, Calif.: RAND Corporation, 2002.

Asch, Beth, and John T. Warner, *An Examination of the Effects of Voluntary Separation Incentives,* Santa Monica, Calif.: RAND Corporation, 2001.

Buddin, Richard, *Success of First-Term Soldiers*, Santa Monica, Calif.: RAND Corporation, 2005.

Buddin, Richard, Daniel S. Levy, Janet M. Hanley, and Donald M. Waldman, *Promotion Tempo and Enlisted Retention*, Santa Monica, Calif.: RAND Corporation, 1992.

Buddin, Richard, and D. Phuong Do, *Assessing the Personal Financial Problems of Junior Enlisted Personnel*, Santa Monica, Calif.: RAND Corporation, 2002.

Clifford, James, "The Meaning of Indefinite Reenlistment," *The NCO Journal*, Winter 2001, pp. 20–21.

Cymrot, Donald J., and Michael L. Hansen, "Overhauling Enlisted Careers and Compensation," in Cindy Williams, ed., *Filling the Ranks: Transforming the U.S. Military Personnel System*, Cambridge, Mass.: MIT Press, 2004, pp. 119–143.

DACMC. See Defense Advisory Committee on Military Compensation.

Defense Advisory Committee on Military Compensation (DACMC), "Preliminary Findings/Recommendations," January 2006, http://www.defenselink.mil/prhome/docs/dacmc_pre_rec0106.pdf (as of April 25, 2006).

Department of National Defence and Canadian Forces, *From Project Inception to Option Analysis, June 1998–May 2001: Canadian Forces Regular Force Terms of Service (TOS) Review Project*, Vol. I, May 2001.

"Development Changes Affect Chiefs," *Air Force Policy Letter Digest*, February 2004, http://www.af.mil/library/policy/letters/pl2004_02.html #chiefs (as of March 30, 2006).

Ganzeboom, Harry B. G., and Donald J. Treiman, "Internationally Comparable Measures of Occupational Status for the 1988 International Standard Classification of Occupations," *Social Science Research*, Vol. 25, No. 3, September 1996, pp. 201–239.

Gilmore, G. J., *New Program Simplifies Re-Enlistment for Some NCOs*, September 18, 1998, http://www.dcmilitary.com/army/standard/archives/sept18/fd_b91898.html (as of March 30, 2006).

Goodrum, Brent W., "The Marine Corps' Deep Battle: Career Force Retention," n.d., http://www.manpower.usmc.mil/pls/portal/docs/PAGE/M_RA_HOME/MM/A_EA/MMEA64/A_CT/MMEA64_CAREER%20TOOLBOX_REFERENCES/MARINE%20CORPS%20DEEP%20BATTLE.PDF (as of March 30, 2006).

Haltiner, Karl W., and Tibor Szvircsev Tresch, "The Decline of Conscription in Europe: Are There Lessons for the US?" paper presented at the conference "Bearing Arms: Who Should Serve?" New York, Harry Guggenheim Foundation, March 31–April 2, 2005.

Headquarters Air Force Personnel Center (HQ AFPC), "FY04 Force Shaping: HQAFPC/DPPR," Randolph Air Force Base, Tex., n.d.

HQ AFPC. See Headquarters Air Force Personnel Center.

Hosek, James, and Beth Asch, *Air Force Compensation: Considering Some Options for Change*, Santa Monica, Calif.: RAND Corporation, 2002.

Hosek, James R., and Michael G. Mattock, *Learning About Quality: How the Quality of Military Personnel Is Revealed over Time*, Santa Monica, Calif.: RAND Corporation, 2003.

Hosek, James R., Michael G. Mattock, C. Christine Fair, Jennifer Kavanagh, Jennifer Sharp, and Mark Totten, *Attracting the Best: How the Military Competes for Information Technology Personnel*, Santa Monica, Calif.: RAND Corporation, 2004.

Jumper, John, "CSAF Sight Picture: Shaping the Force," *Air Force Policy Letter Digest*, February 2004, http://www.af.mil/library/policy/letters/pl2004_02.html#csaf (as of March 30, 2006).

Kleinhart, C., and A. Nicklaus, *Italy to Create a Professional Army*, Sept. 19, 1999, http://www.wsws.org/articles/1999/sep1999/ital-s24.shtml (as of March 30, 2006).

Krueger, R. A., and M. A. Casey, *Focus Groups: A Practical Guide for Applied Research*, Thousand Oaks, Calif.: Sage Publications, 2000.

Lee, Kibeom, Julie J. Carswell, and Natalie J. Allen, "A Meta-Analytic Review of Occupational Commitment: Relations with Person- and Work-Related Variables, *Journal of Applied Psychology*, Vol. 85. No. 5, 2000, pp. 799–811.

Lee, L. G., "10 Year Reenlistment," memorandum to Sgt. Major of the Army, Master Chief Petty Officer of the Navy, and Master Chief Petty Officer of the Air Force, April 11, 1996.

Lock, Douglas, "The Regular Force Terms of Service (TOS) Review Project, The New Structure: A Primer," Department of National Defence, Canada, April 30, 2004a.

———, "Terms of Service Instruction Comments," draft instruction, Department of National Defence Canada, August 2004b.

———, "Variable Initial Engagement, Annex B," draft instruction, Department of National Defence, Canada, August 2004c.

Manpower and Reserve Affairs Department, "Enlisted Retention Task Force Conference VI" briefing, HQ USMC, Quantico, Va., April 19, 2001.

McCormick, David, *The Downsized Warrior: America's Army in Transition*, New York: New York University Press, 1998.

Miech, Richard A., William Eaton, and Kung-Yee Liang, "Occupational Stratification over the Life Course," *Work and Occupations*, Vol. 30, No. 4, November 2003, pp. 440–473.

Military Police Division [USMC], "Indefinite Expiration of Active Duty (EAS) Status for Staff Noncommissioned Officers (SNCOS)," comment on MMEA-1 r/s, October 18, 2000.

MP Division. See Military Police Division.

National Defense Authorization Act for Fiscal Year 2001, Pub. L. No. 106-398, 114 Stat. 1654, 2000.

Orvis, Bruce, and Beth J. Asch, *Military Recruiting: Trends, Outlook, and Implications*, Santa Monica, Calif.: RAND Corporation, 2001.

Parliament of the Commonwealth of Australia, *Recruitment and Retention of ADF Personnel*, Canberra, Australia: Senate Printing Unit, Parliament House, 2001.

Peck, J. A., and J. C. Martin, *The U.S. Navy's Enlisted Voluntary Indefinite Status Study*, Falls Church, Va.: SAG Corporation, 1995.

Quester, Aline, "Ten-Year Reenlistment Proposal (or Indefinite Obligations for Enlisted Marines with More Than Ten Years of Service)," memorandum for Deputy Chief of Staff for Manpower and Reserve Affairs, U.S. Marine Corps, April 8, 1996.

Quester, Aline, and Gary Lee, "Marines Separated with 10 or More Years of Service: An Update," memorandum for the Assistant Deputy Chief of Staff for Manpower and Reserve Affairs, Alexandria, Va.: Center for Naval Analyses, September 13, 2000.

Representative from the Department of National Defence and Canadian Forces, "New Terms of Service Now in Effect," *Canadian Forces Personnel Newsletter*, Issue 5/05, May 2005, available at http://www.forces.gc.ca/hr/cfpn/engraph/5_05_tos_e.asp.

Representative from the Dutch Ministry of Defense; Integrale Monitor Personeelsvoorziening Defensie, 2002; Dutch Ministry of Defense, 2003.

Representative from Manning (Army) at the United Kingdom Ministry of Defence.

Shukiar, Herbert J., John D. Winkler, and John E. Peters, *Enhancing Retention of Army Noncommissioned Officers*, Santa Monica, Calif.: RAND Corporation, 2000.

Spence, Floyd D., "Statement of Chairman Floyd D. Spence at the Conclusion of the Mark-Up for the Fiscal Year 1997 National Defense Authorization Act," http://www.house.gov/hasc/openingstatementsandpressreleases/104th congress/markupb.htm (as of March 30, 2006).

Stroud, S., and T. Omeltchenko, "The Post–Cold War Environment for National Service Policy: Developments in Germany, Italy and China," in H. Perold, S. Stroud, and M. Sherraden, eds., *Service Enquiry: Service in the 21st Century*, St. Louis, Mo.: Global Services Institute, 2003, http://www.service-enquiry.org.za/first_edition_download.asp (as of March 30, 2006).

Thie, Harry, Margaret C. Harrell, and Marc Thibault, *Officer Sabbaticals: Analysis of Extended Leave Options*, Santa Monica, Calif.: RAND Corporation, 2003.

Thornhill, Adrian, and Mark N. K. Saunders, "The Meanings, Consequences, and Implications of the Management of Downsizing and Redundancy: A Review," *Personnel Review*, Vol. 27, No. 4, 1998, pp. 271–295.

Treiman, Donald, *Occupational Prestige in Comparative Perspective*, New York: Academic Press, 1977, p. 177.

United Kingdom Ministry of Defence, *The White Book*, 2003.

United States General Accounting Office, *Military Personnel: DOD Needs More Effective Controls to Better Assess the Progress of the Selective Reenlistment Bonus Program* (GA-04-86), November 2003.

Warner, John, *Thinking About Military Retirement*, Alexandria, Va.: Center for Naval Analyses, January 2006.

Wegener, Bernd, "Concepts and Measurement of Prestige," *Annual Review of Sociology*, 1992, pp. 253–280.

Wong, Leonard, *Stifling Innovation: Developing Tomorrow's Leaders Today*, Carlisle Barracks, Pa.: Strategic Studies Institute, 2002.

———, *Developing Adaptive Leaders: The Crucible Experience of Operation Iraqi Freedom*, Carlisle Barracks, Pa.: Strategic Studies Institute, 2004.

Zanini, Michele, *Italy's All-Volunteer Army: An Analytical Framework for Understanding the Key Policy Issues and Choices During the Transition*, Santa Monica, Calif.: RAND Corporation, RGSD-162, 2002.

Zech, Lanco W., "Open-Ended Reenlistment Contracts," memorandum to the Chief of Naval Operations, Washington D.C., February 10, 1981.

Zhou, Xeuguang, "The Institutional Logic of Occupational Prestige Ranking: Reconceptualization and Reanalyses," *American Journal of Sociology*, Vol. 111, No. 1, July 2005, pp. 90–140.